HOSTILE TO DEMOCRACY
The Movement System and Political Repression in Uganda

Human Rights Watch
New York • Washington • London • Brussels

ISBN 1-56432-239-4
Library of Congress Catalog Card Number 99-65985

Cover design by Rafael Jiménez
Cover photo ©AP/Wide World Photos

Addresses for Human Rights Watch
350 Fifth Avenue, 34th Floor, New York, NY 10118-3299
Tel: (212) 290-4700, Fax: (212) 736-1300, E-mail: hrwnyc@hrw.org

1522 K Street, N.W., #910, Washington, DC 20005-1202
Tel: (202) 371-6592, Fax: (202) 371-0124, E-mail: hrwdc@hrw.org

33 Islington High Street, N1 9LH London, UK
Tel: (171) 713-1995, Fax: (171) 713-1800, E-mail: hrwatchuk@gn.apc.org

15 Rue Van Campenhout, 1000 Brussels, Belgium
Tel: (2) 732-2009, Fax: (2) 732-0471, E-mail:hrwatcheu@skynet.be

Web Site Address: http://www.hrw.org

Listserv address: To subscribe to the list, send an e-mail message to
majordomo@igc.apc.org with "subscribe hrw-news" in the body of the message
(leave the subject line blank).

Human Rights Watch is dedicated to
protecting the human rights of people around the world.

We stand with victims and activists to prevent
discrimination, to uphold political freedom, to protect people from inhumane
conduct in wartime, and to bring offenders to justice.

We investigate and expose
human rights violations and hold abusers accountable.

We challenge governments and those who hold power to end abusive practices
and respect international human rights law.

We enlist the public and the international
community to support the cause of human rights for all.

HUMAN RIGHTS WATCH

Human Rights Watch conducts regular, systematic investigations of human rights abuses in some seventy countries around the world. Our reputation for timely, reliable disclosures has made us an essential source of information for those concerned with human rights. We address the human rights practices of governments of all political stripes, of all geopolitical alignments, and of all ethnic and religious persuasions. Human Rights Watch defends freedom of thought and expression, due process and equal protection of the law, and a vigorous civil society; we document and denounce murders, disappearances, torture, arbitrary imprisonment, discrimination, and other abuses of internationally recognized human rights. Our goal is to hold governments accountable if they transgress the rights of their people.

Human Rights Watch began in 1978 with the founding of its Europe and Central Asia division (then known as Helsinki Watch). Today, it also includes divisions covering Africa, the Americas, Asia, and the Middle East. In addition, it includes three thematic divisions on arms, children's rights, and women's rights. It maintains offices in New York, Washington, Los Angeles, London, Brussels, Moscow, Dushanbe, Rio de Janeiro, and Hong Kong. Human Rights Watch is an independent, nongovernmental organization, supported by contributions from private individuals and foundations worldwide. It accepts no government funds, directly or indirectly.

The staff includes Kenneth Roth, executive director; Michele Alexander, development director; Reed Brody, advocacy director; Carroll Bogert, communications director; Cynthia Brown, program director; Barbara Guglielmo, finance and administration director; Jeri Laber, special advisor; Lotte Leicht, Brussels office director; Patrick Midges, publications director; Susan Osnos, associate director; Jemera Rone, counsel; Wilder Tayler, general counsel; and Joanna Weschler, United Nations representative. Jonathan Fanton is the chair of the board. Robert L. Bernstein is the founding chair.

The regional directors of Human Rights Watch are Peter Takirambudde, Africa; José Miguel Vivanco, Americas; Sidney Jones, Asia; Holly Cartner, Europe and Central Asia; and Hanny Megally, Middle East and North Africa. The thematic division directors are Joost R. Hiltermann, arms; Lois Whitman, children's; and Regan Ralph, women's.

The members of the board of directors are Jonathan Fanton, chair; Lisa Anderson, Robert L. Bernstein, William Carmichael, Dorothy Cullman, Gina Despres, Irene Diamond, Adrian W. DeWind, Fiona Druckenmiller, Edith Everett, Michael E. Gellert, Vartan Gregorian, Alice H. Henkin, James F. Hoge, Stephen L. Kass, Marina Pinto Kaufman, Bruce Klatsky, Josh Mailman, Yolanda T. Moses, Samuel K. Murumba, Andrew Nathan, Jane Olson, Peter Osnos, Kathleen Peratis, Bruce Rabb, Sigrid Rausing, Orville Schell, Sid Sheinberg, Gary G. Sick, Malcolm Smith, Domna Stanton, and Maya Wiley. Robert L. Bernstein is the founding chair of Human Rights Watch.

ACKNOWLEDGMENTS

This report is based on a five-week fact-finding mission to Uganda conducted by Peter Bouckaert, Uganda researcher in the Africa Division of Human Rights Watch, during April and May 1998. Jemera Rone, associate counsel, participated in the fact-finding mission to western and northern Uganda. Additional research was conducted in Uganda by Peter Bouckaert in May 1999. The report was written by Peter Bouckaert. Elizabeth Brundige, Everett intern in the Children's Rights Division, drafted the section on children and treason charges. Jemera Rone, Binaifer Nowrojee, counsel to the Africa division, and Bronwen Manby, counsel to the Africa division, Wilder Tayler, general counsel, and Michael McClintock, deputy program director, edited the report. Members of the Africa Division's Advisory Committee Edward Kannyo, Muna Ndulo, James C. N. Paul, Aristide R. Zolberg, Michael Chege, and Arthur C. Helton also contributed comments. Zachary Freeman, Associate for the Africa Division, prepared the report for production.

Human Rights Watch wishes to thank the human rights activists, academics, political activists, humanitarian workers, and government officials who contributed to this report. Without their efforts and assistance, this report would have been impossible. Most importantly, Human Rights Watch wishes to thank the victims and witnesses of human rights abuses who agreed to share their experiences with us, in the hope that the human rights record of Uganda will be improved.

TABLE OF CONTENTS

ACRONYMS

ADF	Allied Democratic Forces
DP	Democratic Party
ESO	External Security Organization
FAD	Foundation for African Development
FHRI	Foundation for Human Rights Initiative
FOWODE	Forum for Women in Democracy
FRONESA	Front for National Salvation
HRC	Uganda Human Rights Commission
ICCPR	International Covenant on Civil and Political Rights
IFES	International Foundation for Election Systems
ISO	Internal Security Organization
LC	Local Councils, formerly known as Resistance Councils (RC)
LDU	Local Defense Unit
LRA/M	Lord's Resistance Army/Movement
Chaka-mchaka	Program of political and military education instituted by the NRM government to promote the movement political system.
NDF	National Democrats Forum
NOCEM	National Organization for Civic Education and Elections Monitoring
NRM/A	The National Resistance Movement/Army, subsequently renamed the UPDF
RDC	Resident District Commissioners
SPLM/A	The Sudanese People's Liberation Movement/Army
Tabliq	An Islamic group, also known as Jamaat Daawa Assalafiya. Some radical elements of the Tabliq group are suspected of involvement in the ADF rebel movement
UDHR	Universal Declaration on Human Rights
UHEDOC	Uganda Human Rights Education and Documentation Center
UNA	Uganda National Army
UNICEF	United Nations Childrens' Fund
UNLA	Uganda National Liberation Army
UNRF II	Uganda National Rescue Front II
UPC	Uganda People's Congress
UPM	Uganda Patriotic Movement
UPDA	Uganda People's Democratic Army
UPDF	Uganda People's Defense Force
UYD	Uganda Young Democrats
WFP	World Food Program

Unlike the law of Moses, most human rights are not divinely ordained and are subject to modification to fit the political and socio-economic conditions of the societies where they are applied.

President Yoweri Museveni, speaking at Liberation Day celebrations in Kampala, January 26, 1999.

Fundamental rights and freedoms of the individual are inherent and not granted by the State.

Uganda Constitution (1995), Article 20 (1).

I. SUMMARY

When Yoweri Museveni and his National Resistance Army/Movement (NRA/M) took the reigns of power in Uganda after a five-year-long guerrilla war, Uganda was a country infamous for massive civilian killings and other human rights abuses on an enormous scale. During the military dictatorship of Idi Amin (1971-1979) and after the return to power of Milton Obote in 1980, hundreds of thousands of civilians were killed and many more were subjected to arbitrary arrest, beatings, torture, and other abuse.

The NRA/NRM took power in 1986 on a platform promising a "fundamental revolution" and not "a mere change of the guard."[1] Since then, the NRM has enjoyed a virtual monopoly on political power in Uganda. Through a carefully managed political system, the NRM has been able to effectively neutralize political opposition which it characterizes as sectarian, divisive, and at odds with national unity.

In some areas, the human rights record of Uganda has improved significantly since the NRM took power. Although police and army abuse persist, the NRM has forged an army which is more disciplined and more conscious of the rights of civilians than its predecessors. Relative stability has returned to some areas of the country, but violent conflicts continue in the west and north of Uganda. The empowerment of women has been a key goal of the NRM administration, and the NRM administration has significantly increased the voice of women in government. The Uganda Human Rights Commission, established in 1996, has taken its mandate seriously and has investigated many human rights abuses. The change which has taken place in these and other areas is indisputable, and much appreciated by the majority of the Ugandan population. The steps taken by the Ugandan government to improve its human rights record deserve praise, and show more than a cosmetic commitment to human rights.

But the progressive policies pursued by the NRM in some areas of human rights protection contrast sharply with its policies in the political arena. Organized political activity has been outlawed in Uganda for the past twelve years, and the NRM government has not hesitated to resort to repressive measures when these legal restrictions on political activity are challenged. Numerous political rallies have been halted, some through force. Political activists who have challenged the NRM's hold on political power are frequently harassed and sometimes arbitrarily arrested. The NRM has demonized political parties, blaming them for all the

---

[1] President Yoweri Katunga Museveni, *Sowing the Mustard Seed* (London: MacMillian, 1997), p. 172.

abuses of the past in Uganda, although the NRM is itself to any outsider just that—a political party.

Human Rights Watch researchers traveled to Uganda in April and May 1998 to assess the human rights dimensions of the NRM's "no-party" or "movement" system of government and to document human rights abuses associated with the NRM's long monopoly of government. Abuses by the Lord's Resistance Army (LRA), a rebel group operating in northern Uganda, were documented in Human Rights Watch's 1997 report, *Scars of Death*. This report focuses on the "movement" political system, analyzing its legal structures and actual operation against international human rights standards.

Legal Restrictions on Civil and Political Rights

A complex web of legal restrictions limits political opposition in Uganda. The new Ugandan constitution, adopted in 1995, allows political parties to exist in name but outlaws all the activities normally associated with political parties. Political organizations are prohibited from opening and operating branch offices, holding delegates' conferences, and holding public rallies. Political organizations are further prohibited from "sponsoring or offering a platform to or in any way campaigning for or against a candidate for any public elections." Finally, a vague clause prohibits political organizations from "carrying on any activities that may interfere with the movement political system for the time being in force."

The severe restrictions on independent political activity contained in the constitution will ultimately be supplemented by the Political Organizations Bill currently being considered by parliament. The draft currently under consideration maintains many of the severe restrictions on political rights. The bill would also create many obstacles for parties seeking the required registration, including high registration fees and requirements such as having founding members in one-third of Uganda's districts.

The Political Organizations Bill, if enacted, will not regulate political parties, but rather restrict them to the point of ineffectiveness. Many of the restrictions on political party activities currently in article 269 of the constitution are maintained. Political parties will continue to be prohibited from sponsoring or offering a platform to any candidate seeking electoral office, although the ruling NRM will continue to be able to do so. Severe sanctions are provided for any violation of the provisions of the bill.

The Movement System: Towards a One-Party State in Uganda?

Only one political organization in Uganda is exempted from the strict regulations placed on political activity in Uganda: the ruling National Resistance

Movement (NRM). The NRM has effectively excluded itself from regulation by characterizing itself not as a political party but as a "movement," fusing its structures with those of the Ugandan state, and creating a pyramid of "movement" structures from the village level to the national level. All Ugandans belong to the "movement," even those who oppose it: compulsory membership that is itself inconsistent with the right *not* to be forced to belong to an association. The "movement" structures are state-funded and are administered at the national level by a National Political Commissar, who is responsible for the political mobilization and education of the population. By denying that the NRM is a political party, the NRM avoids being forced to comply with the regulations imposed on opposition political parties, and by fusing its structures with the Ugandan state the NRM gains direct access to state funds and the powers of state mobilization. Since the NRM is not officially a political party, despite having the characteristics of a ruling political party in a single-party state, it has sought to create the illusion that Uganda is a "no-party" state. Such semantics obscure the basic reality of the NRM's partisan dominance of the political process in Uganda.

The "movement" posts filled by the July 1998 elections are not the only structures used by the NRM to influence public opinion and mobilize public support. Since coming to power, the NRM has used a state-funded program of political and military education called *chaka-mchaka* to spread its message that political parties are destructive sectarian organizations responsible for Uganda's past woes, an argument that resonates given Uganda's recent political history. *Chaka-mchaka* thus serves to rationalize the NRM's denial of political rights of freedom of expression, association, and assembly. Government leaders, including President Museveni, often refer to advocates of democratic reform as their "enemies." Other structures of local government such as the local councils (LC) and the Resident District Commissioners (RDC) serve to ensure support for the NRM, and often create a hostile climate for advocates of pluralism.

In the year 2000, the NRM-dominated government plans to have a public referendum on whether to continue with the "movement" system or return to a more pluralist political system. Because the referendum would effectively put internationally recognized human rights of freedom of association and assembly up for a vote, it is incompatible with human rights standards. Human rights are universal, and not subject to a majority mandate. It is also difficult to envision a fair and free referendum on the question of political parties in Uganda because the NRM remains in almost complete control of the government and has extensively used state funding to spread its message against independent political parties. Because the stringent limitations on their activities remain in force, independent political parties are deprived from mounting an effective public campaign on the referendum. It is doubtful whether the NRM is willing to create the environment in which a free and fair referendum could take place. Most advocates for pluralism in Uganda view the referendum as the final step in a carefully constructed consolidation of power by the NRM, and have refused to participate in the referendum.

Violations of the Rights to Freedom of Association and Assembly

The Ugandan government has vigorously enforced the ban on political activities independent of the NRM. Opposition activists and civil society representatives in Uganda documented many cases in which meetings deemed political were dispersed by the Ugandan authorities. Around the time of U.S. President Bill Clinton's visit to Uganda in March 1998, at least two political events were broken up or prevented by police. In May 1998, the Ugandan authorities halted a seminar discussing the controversial Land Bill, and arrested two members of parliament following a rally opposing the bill. In June and July, 1998, at least four seminars sponsored by the Foundation for African Development (FAD) and the Uganda Young Democrats (UYD) on the topic of "Human Rights and Democracy" were dispersed by the police, some violently. At a June 19, 1998, FAD/UYD seminar in Tororo, six persons were injured after the police charged into the building and beat participants with batons.

The Ugandan authorities also blocked a UYD rally in Mbarara on July 21, 1998; a seminar on the land act sponsored by the Young Congress of Uganda, a group aligned with the Uganda People's Congress (UPC) political party, in Mbale on July 25, 1988; and an August 9, 1998, seminar in Iganga at which the president of the Justice Forum, Kibirige Mayanja, was supposed to speak on poverty alleviation in Uganda. A paralegal workshop sponsored in Masindi on July 27, 1998, by the Foundation for Human Rights Initiative (FHRI), the largest human rights organization in Uganda, was almost dispersed because the resident district commissioner had confused the organization with the FAD.

In December 1998, Karuhanga Chapaa, chair of the National Democrats Forum (NDF), was arrested and charged with sedition in connection with anti-Museveni comments he allegedly made at a political rally. Chapaa claims he was misquoted in the newspaper article about the rally. He was convicted of sedition in June 1999, and plans to appeal. After allegedly attending another political event at Bitereko on December 26, 1998, Chapaa received a threatening letter from the resident district commissioner, ordering him to stop engaging in "illegal political activities" and suggesting that Chapaa had uttered "treasonable utterances." The letter also ordered Chapaa to stop distributing party membership cards, "which is an illegal act."

On January 6, 1999, the house of Wasswa Lule, a member of Parliament, was surrounded in the evening by heavily-armed policemen and he was arrested and taken to the Kampala police station. At the police station, Lule was interrogated about having suggested at a seminar that President Museveni should be personally probed for involvement in corruption. Lule was released at about 2 a.m., and was not charged with an offense.

On January 16, 1999, three FAD officials were arrested in the West Nile town of Moyo while participating in a training seminar on civic education. The training seminar was dispersed by the police. The district police commander demanded that the FAD officials write a letter of apology before releasing them twenty-eight hours after the arrest. On April 26, 1999, police and intelligence officials harassed and intimated a local council chairperson in Mpingi district who had allowed FAD to organize a workshop on "Human Rights in the Community." The officials warned the local council chairperson not to give FAD access to such forums in the district.

Political parties are prohibited from holding party conferences, a ban which severely hampers their own internal reform. Since this ban has been in place since 1986, reform in the structure and leadership of political parties has been virtually impossible. Attempts to hold party conferences have been met with strong and unambiguous warnings from the Ugandan government that they would prevent such meetings. The restrictions have also made it virtually impossible for viable independent political parties to emerge, and have hampered attempts at internal reform among the existing parties.

Restrictions on Civil Society and the Media

Uganda has an active and diverse civil society and a vibrant media. The Uganda Human Rights Network (HURINET) has twenty-five member organizations. Uganda is home to a number of independent newspapers and radio and television stations, including some which are highly critical of government policies. Despite this partial openness, however, the government continues to interfere with the work of human rights groups and the media in Uganda.

The government exercises considerable control over nongovernmental organizations (NGOs) by delaying or threatening to withdraw their registration, which must be sanctioned by a government-controlled board and can be quickly revoked. Although the NGO Registration Statute sets no such requirements, NGOs must function as nonpolitical and nonsectarian organizations, and practice a significant amount of self-censorship of their programs in order to obtain and maintain registration. Some NGOs have faced significant interference from the Ugandan government. The government has refused to register the Uganda National NGO Forum since 1997, and declared its 1999 second general assembly an "illegal meeting." The National Organization for Civic Education and Elections Monitoring (NOCEM), a coalition of twelve NGOs which sought to engage in civic education and election monitoring, had to wait almost three years for its registration, apparently because the government was concerned that the organization included advocates of democratic pluralism. The Uganda Human Rights Education and Documentation Center (UHEDOC) had its registration arbitrarily terminated after hosting a widely attended seminar on corruption in Uganda. The Ugandan government has also attempted to create its own NRM-aligned civil society structures and is hostile to attempts by NGOs to organize themselves into more effective networks. President Museveni has often reacted with hostility to accusations of government abuse of human rights by NGOs, urging them to focus on rebel abuses instead.

Although it allows a vocal and independent press, the Ugandan government continues to regularly detain, interrogate, and criminally charge journalists for their reporting. Common charges include the publication of false news and seditious libel, under legislation dating from the colonial era. More commonly, journalists are called in to police stations and interrogated about particular press reports, to be released hours later without charges. Since 1995, the editors of the *Monitor*, *Citizen*, *Crusader,* the *People*, *Rupiny*, *Uganda Express*, *Uganda Confidential*, *Assalaam*, and *Shariat* have all been detained and questioned about stories in their respective papers, and some have been charged with criminal offenses. Hussein Musa Njuki, editor of the Islamic opposition paper *Assalaam*, died in police custody in August 1995 under unclear circumstances. The frequent arrest and harassment of journalists has a chilling effect on freedom of the press in Uganda, causing many journalists to practice self-censorship. The media is also strictly controlled through the 1995 Press and Journalists Law which grants the government Media Council the power to suspend journalists and publications.

Abuse of Treason Charges

The charge of treason, one of the most serious in any criminal system, carries a mandatory death sentence in Uganda. Despite its gravity, it is abused as a convenient holding charge, providing for the incarceration of a suspect on remand for up to 360 days without bail. More than 1,000 persons, most of them from rebel areas of Uganda, are currently incarcerated in Uganda awaiting trial on treason charges. While the charge is brought in cases of suspected involvement in one of Uganda's several armed rebel groups, treason charges have also provided the basis for the detention of non-violent political dissidents.

In areas of rebel conflict, torture of treason suspects by soldiers of the Ugandan army (the Uganda People's Defense Force, UPDF) appears widespread.

Treason suspects arrested in Western Uganda, an area destabilized by the ADF rebellion, gave consistent testimony of torture by UPDF soldiers, and some showed researchers injuries which were consistent with their testimonies. The torture included putting sticks between the fingers, tying the hands together and then beating down on them with stones; extensive beatings with heavy canes; and in one case burning the skin of the suspect. Torture was used to extract confessions, which then formed the basis for their incarceration. Interviews with police officials suggested that little active investigation of suspects held on treason charges was taking place. In the words of one police official: "You can get arrested for nothing and there is nothing you can do about it. We feel sorry for them, but it is like catching a stray bullet in a war zone."

A number of leading opposition politicians have been charged with treason by the government. Although treason charges against prominent politicians have decreased, the continued widespread and unchecked bringing of treason charges against ordinary people creates a high level of insecurity, especially in rural areas where people are caught between the terrifying violence of armed opposition groups like the LRA and the suspicions of government troops. People are thus reluctant to express political opinions contrary to the NRM in these areas.

The Role of the International Community

While vigorously advocating democratic reform and respect for civil and political rights elsewhere in Africa, the international community has remained remarkably quiet on abuses of political rights in Uganda. The United States has on occasion called for a more pluralistic democratic system in Uganda and spoken out about the need to respect fundamental rights such as the rights to freedom of expression, association, and assembly. However, these calls have rarely been followed up by action, and have had little impact on the human rights situation in Uganda.

Most other influential nations, such as the United Kingdom, have been even more muted in their comments on the NRM's hold on power, ignoring abuses and restrictions on political rights altogether in favor of an amicable relationship with President Museveni and the Ugandan government. The virtual silence of the international community, while pouring millions of dollars of aid into Uganda, has served as an endorsement of the restrictive movement political system. The United Kingdom and other countries have expressed support for the referendum on political rights scheduled for the year 2000 despite the fact that the referendum will be a vote on the continued suspension of fundamental rights, and is unlikely to take place in a free and fair environment.

Why has the international community remained largely quiet about the abuse of civil and political rights in Uganda? In the view of some Western leaders, President Museveni is a crucial leader in the Great Lakes region and a power broker in regional conflicts, including helping to end the 1994 Rwandan genocide and supporting Zairian rebels in their struggle to topple the Mobutu government in 1997. His role in containing the Islamist government of Sudan through support for the Sudanese rebel Sudanese Peoples' Liberation Army (SPLA) is also in line with the policy objectives of some Western leaders. The NRM administration has ushered in significant economic growth and relative stability, rebuilding Uganda from the wreckage left by the brutal governments of Idi Amin and Milton Obote.

The international community evaluates the human rights record of Museveni's government favorably in relation to the dismal and discouraging records of its predecessors and of most of its neighbors. Thus the human rights abuses which continue to take place under the movement system go largely unremarked and unchallenged by donor countries. Finally, President's Museveni's slogan of "African solutions to African problems" has been embraced by the international community as a means to relinquish its responsibility to address conflict in Africa.

But the acquiescence of the international community to human rights abuses in Uganda serves to undermine respect for human rights both there and elsewhere on the African continent, and indeed worldwide. When human rights abuses are ignored in one country, it becomes more difficult to criticize human rights abuses in others. Without constructive international pressure, it is likely that the NRM government in Uganda will continue to consolidate its grasp on power and repress the political opposition. It is unlikely that the initiative for democratic reform will come from inside the NRM-dominated government without significant international pressure.

II. RECOMMENDATIONS

To the Ugandan Government

- The NRM and the "movement" structures should be considered a political organization and regulated in the same fashion as all other political organizations or parties: they should not be exempted from regulations governing political activity. The government should not fund the NRM, its secretariat, the aligned "movement" structures, or the political campaigns of NRM candidates unless equivalent funding is provided to other political organizations. A strict division should be made between the functioning of the government and the NRM.

- Amend the constitution to remove articles 269, 270, and all other constitutional restrictions on political rights which are inconsistent with international human rights law.

- Respect the right to form political parties without undue government interference, and to engage in political party activities such as, for example, the holding of delegate conferences and political rallies, the sponsoring of candidates for public office, and issuing of party membership cards. Immediately lift all legal and administrative obstacles hindering the registration and functioning of existing and new political parties.

- Revise the draft Political Organizations Bill to make it consistent with international human rights standards. Regulations imposed on political parties should guarantee the rights of free expression and association, and ensure the rights of all Ugandans to participate in their own governance. Regulation should not undermine the ability of political parties to function effectively.

- Respect the right to freedom of association and assembly and halt arbitrary police actions to ban or disperse peaceful public meetings and demonstrations. Desist using charges such as treason, sedition, "promoting sectarianism," and "holding a meeting without a permit" to criminalize and punish peaceful political activity or dissent.

- Recognize the right to form and operate nongovernmental organizations, and refrain from using the licensing process to intimidate or punish nongovernmental organizations. Lift legal and administrative obstacles hindering the registration of nongovernmental organizations.

- Immediately end state funding and other forms of official support for the NRM's chaka-mchaka political education programs, which advance the view that political parties are responsible for Uganda's past troubles and serve to justify violations of civil and political rights in Uganda.

- Cease harassment and arbitrary detention of journalists, and amend legislation governing the media to bring it in line with international norms guaranteeing freedom of expression.

- Provide government, police, army (UPDF) and other officials with special training on human rights standards and protection. Institute procedures that ensure the effective investigation and criminal prosecution of violations of human rights, including violations of the political rights of freedom of expression, association, and assembly.

- Release or bring promptly to trial all persons detained on treason or other security related charges who have been in detention for longer than the constitutionally permitted period of 360 days. Revise the constitutional limit on pre-trial detention, which currently allows for the detention on remand for a period up to 360 days in capital cases.

- All cases of treason suspects should be promptly reviewed to ensure that sufficient evidence exists to justify detention.

- Cease using treason charges as a holding charge for those arbitrarily detained in areas in which rebels are active. Undertake a prompt and comprehensive review of national legislation governing treason, terrorism, and other public order charges to ensure compliance with international human rights standards. In particular:

    - no arrests should take place without sufficient evidence. The current practice of "arrest now, investigate later," is unacceptable.

    -the use of confessions as a basis for pre-trial detention should be limited to confessions freely made in the presence of counsel.

    -suspects should in general be granted bail and a fair and timely trial. Pre-trial detention should be kept to a minimum.

-the independence of the judiciary and law enforcement agencies, including from interference by the army, should be guaranteed.

To the Uganda Human Rights Commission

- In addition to its current monitoring work, the Uganda Human Rights Commission should also closely monitor and regularly report on violations of the right to freedom of expression, association, and assembly. The Human Rights Commission should become a vigorous advocate for the implementation of these internationally recognized rights.

To the International Community

- The international community should use clear benchmarks to advocate and measure progress on human rights, including democratic participation in governance. These benchmarks should be applied consistently. The benchmarks used to measure progress on respect for basic human rights in Uganda should include:

  - lifting of the legal and administrative restrictions on non-NRM political activity;

  - extension of guarantees of freedom of assembly, association, and expression to political parties, nongovernmental organizations, and civil society in general;

  - improvement in the human rights conduct of the army (UPDF), police and other security agencies. In particular, a cessation of torture and the indiscriminate bringing of security-related charges such as "treason" to prolong arbitrary detention; and,

  - separation of the NRM political organization and aligned partisan structures from the government of Uganda, and cessation of public funding for NRM-aligned bodies such as the movement structures.

- Diplomatic representatives should meet regularly with NGO, media, and other civil society representatives to discuss human rights problems. Diplomatic representatives should be encouraged to publicly denounce abuses of human rights in Uganda, including abuses of freedom of expression, association, and assembly. Respect for human rights should be a constant theme of discussion

between the international community and the Ugandan government, in both
public and private interaction.

- Financial assistance, particularly balance of payments support, should be tied
  to the Ugandan government's achievement of clear and firm human rights
  benchmarks. While conditionality is an important human rights instrument,
  the international community should also use dialogue and positive measures
  to encourage change and improvement in human rights observance.
  Humanitarian and development aid should remain unconditional. Poverty
  alleviation should be furthered and encouraged.

- If aid is given, it should include assistance for the development of a pluralistic
  and independent civil society, a vibrant NGO community and human rights
  groups with a monitoring capacity, an independent and accountable press, an
  independent judiciary with the capacity to function effectively, and a robust
  and independent human rights commission.

- Provide human rights training as an integral component of all capacity
  building and training projects involving the Ugandan police, the UPDF or
  other security organizations. Such training should include a strong
  component designed to stop the use of torture and other cruel, inhuman, and
  degrading treatment as an interrogation technique. Human rights training
  should be incorporated into all internationally sponsored military training
  programs in Uganda.

To the Commonwealth and its Member States
- Monitor respect for human rights in Uganda, in particular respect for the
  political rights of freedom of expression, association, and assembly. Issue
  statements condemning violations of human rights in Uganda, and urge the
  Ugandan government to adopt the necessary reforms to meet its international
  human rights obligations.

- Call upon the Commonwealth Secretariat to carry out a study of violations of
  human rights associated with the movement system in Uganda, and to
  propose appropriate action by the Commonwealth nations on this issue.

III. INTRODUCTION

When Yoweri Museveni and his National Resistance Army/Movement (NRA/M) took the reigns of power in Uganda after a five-year-long guerrilla war, Uganda was a country infamous for massive civilian killings and other human rights abuses on an enormous scale. During the military dictatorship of Idi Amin (1971-1979) and after the return to power of Milton Obote in 1980, hundreds of thousands of civilians were killed and many more were subjected to arbitrary arrest, beatings, torture, and other abuse.

The NRA/NRM took power in 1986 on a platform promising a "fundamental revolution" and not "a mere change of the guard."[2] Since then, the NRM has enjoyed a virtual monopoly on political power in Uganda. Through a carefully managed political system, the NRM has been able to effectively neutralize political opposition which it characterizes as sectarian, divisive, and at odds with national unity.

In some areas, the human rights record of Uganda has improved significantly since the NRM took power. Although police and army abuse persist, the NRM has forged an army which is more disciplined and more conscious of the rights of civilians than its predecessors. Relative stability has returned to some areas of the country, but violent conflicts continue in the west and north of Uganda. The empowerment of women has been a key goal of the NRM administration, and the NRM administration has significantly increased the voice of women in government. The Uganda Human Rights Commission, established in 1996, has taken its mandate seriously and has investigated many human rights abuses. The change which has taken place in these and other areas is indisputable, and much appreciated by the majority of the Ugandan population. The steps taken by the Ugandan government to improve its human rights record deserve praise, and show more than a cosmetic commitment to human rights.

But the progressive policies pursued by the NRM in some areas of human rights protection contrast sharply with its policies in the political arena. Organized political activity has been outlawed in Uganda for the past twelve years, and the NRM government has not hesitated to resort to repressive measures when these legal restrictions on political activity are challenged. Numerous political rallies have been halted, some through force. Political activists who have challenged the NRM's hold on political power are frequently harassed and sometimes arbitrarily arrested. The NRM has demonized political parties, blaming them for all the

---

[2]President Yoweri Katunga Museveni, *Sowing the Mustard Seed* (London: MacMillian, 1997), p. 172.

abuses of the past in Uganda, although it is itself to any outsider just that—a political party.

Human Rights Watch researchers traveled to Uganda in April and May 1998 to assess the human rights dimensions of the NRM's "no-party" or "movement" system of government and to document human rights abuses associated with the NRM's long monopoly of government. Abuses by the Lord's Resistance Army (LRA), a rebel group operating in northern Uganda, were documented in Human Rights Watch's 1997 report, *Scars of Death*. This report focuses on the "movement" political system, analyzing its legal structures and actual operation against international human rights standards.

IV. UGANDA'S OBLIGATIONS UNDER INTERNATIONAL LAW

The Ugandan government often responds to criticisms of what it calls the "movement" system by arguing that such criticisms are insensitive to the Ugandan context, and a form of western imperialism. Such a response differs little from that of other governments dominated by leaders of long incumbency and single parties, and cannot be expected to silence critics either within Uganda or abroad. Many concerns raised about the movement system arise from its violations of civil and political rights enshrined in United Nations treaties and conventions, not from some inflexible Western notion of proper forms of democracy. Democracy takes many forms, even within the Western world. But the world community, through various international instruments such as the Universal Declaration of Human Rights and the International Covenant on Civil and Political Rights (ICCPR), has set certain standards to which all signatory governments are expected to adhere.[3]

Uganda acceded to the ICCPR on June 21, 1995, without making any reservations. The Ugandan government is under the obligation to respect and protect the internationally recognized human rights contained therein. This report evaluates Uganda's political system and related human rights practices in light of these international standards.

Two of the main arguments the Ugandan government often advances in defense of its restrictions on civil and political rights are that the restrictions on political rights have been adopted by mandate of the majority, and that these restrictions should be seen in the context of Uganda's advancements in other areas of human rights and development.

Human rights are not subject to majority mandate. The very purpose and origins of human rights law were to place certain fundamental rights beyond the whims of majority opinion, and to protect those who may find themselves in the minority. The permissible grounds for derogation from human rights obligations are listed in the international instruments themselves, and derogation by majority consensus is clearly not envisioned.

Neither should Uganda's achievements in other areas of human rights and development detract from its international obligations to respect and enforce human rights such as freedom of association, assembly, and expression. All human rights serve a recognized purpose, and allowing governments to pick and choose those

---

[3]The Universal Declaration of Human Rights is not a treaty to which states become parties by signing the document, but is considered an authoritative statement on human rights; it is almost universally accepted that membership in the United Nations entails adherence to its principles.

human rights which they wish to enforce while ignoring other obligations would be counter to the very purpose of human rights law.

Freedom of Association

Freedom of association is guaranteed by Article 22(1) of the ICCPR, which provides that "Everyone shall have the right to freedom of association with others, including the right to form and join trade unions for the protection of his interests."[4] The scope of the right to freedom of association is broad, and includes the right to form political parties.[5] The right to freedom of association and the right not to be compelled to belong to any association are also recognized in the African [Banjul] Charter on Human and People's Rights.[6] The Universal Declaration of Human Rights also recognizes the right to freedom of association, and further requires that "[n]o one may be compelled to belong to an association."[7]

The right to freedom of association is a fundamental human right and indispensable for the existence and functioning of democracy, as explained by the noted scholar Dr. Manfred Nowak:

> As a *political right*, [freedom of association] is indispensable for the existence and functioning of democracy, because political interests can be effectively championed *only in community with others* (as a political party, professional interest group, organization or other association for pursuing particular public interests).[8]

The right to free association imposes on governments the obligation to permit and guarantee the organization of all political parties, according to the Inter-American Commission on Human Rights, interpreting the free association provision in the American Convention on Human Rights.[9]

---

[4]ICCPR, Article 21(1).

[5]Dr. Manfred Nowak, *U.N. Covenant on Civil and Political Rights: CCPR Commentary* (Kehl: N.P. Engel, 1993), p. 386; Karl Joseph Partsch, "Freedom of Conscience and Expression, Political Freedoms," in Louis Henkin (ed.), *The International Bill of Rights: The Covenant on Civil and Political Rights* (New York: Columbia University Press, 1981), p. 235.

[6]African [Banjul] Charter on Human and People's Rights, Article 10.

[7]Universal Declaration of Human Rights, Article 20(2).

[8]Nowak, *CCPR Commentary*, p. 385 (second emphasis added).

[9]American Convention on Human Rights, Article 16: "1. Everyone has the right to associate freely for ideological, religious, political, economic, labor, social, cultural, sports, or other purposes. 2. The exercise of this right shall be subject only to such restrictions

Restrictions on the right to freedom of association under the ICCPR must be prescribed by law and "necessary in a democratic society," and "in the interest of national security or public safety, public order (*ordre public*), the protection of public health or morals or the protection of the rights and freedoms of others."[10] A ban on political parties is scarcely "necessary in a democratic society" since historically the development of democracy has been inextricably linked to political parties contesting power through free and fair elections in an atmosphere of free speech and assembly.

Derogation from the right to freedom of association and some other rights is permissible only under the circumstances set forth in Article 4 of the ICCPR:

> 1. In time of public emergency which threatens the life of the nation and the existence of which is officially proclaimed, the States Parties to the present Covenant may take measures derogating from their obligations under the present Covenant to the extent strictly required by the exigencies of the situation, provided that such measures are not inconsistent with their other obligations under international law and do not involve discrimination solely on the ground of race, color, sex, language, religion or social origin.

---

established by law as may be necessary in a democratic society, in the interest of national security, public safety or public order, or to protect public health or morals or the rights and freedoms of others."

The Inter-American Commission on Human Rights interpreted this right as meaning that governments have:

> the obligation to permit and guarantee: the organization of all political parties and other associations, unless they are constituted to violate human rights; open debate of the principal theses of socioeconomic development; the celebration of general and free elections with all the necessary guarantees so that the results represent the popular will.

The Inter-American Commission further stated that "[t]he right to political participation makes possible the right to organize parties and political associations, which through open discussion and ideological struggle, can improve the social level and economic circumstances of the masses and prevent a monopoly of power by any group or individual." The right to organize political parties is also derived from the right to participate in government and to free elections, recognized in Article 25 of the ICCPR. Inter-American Commission on Human Rights, *10 Years of Activities: 1971-1981* (Washington, D.C.: General Secretariat, Organization of American States, 1982), pp. 335, 334.

[10]ICCPR, Article 21(2).

2. No derogation from articles 6, 7, 8 (paragraphs 1 and 2), 15, 16 and
18 may be made under this provision.

The public emergency contemplated in Article 4(1) should be of such a magnitude
as to threaten the life of the nation as a whole, whose seriousness is beyond doubt.[11]
The measures which are adopted for derogating from obligations under the ICCPR
are permissible only to the extent that they are strictly required by the exigencies
of the emergency.

The state party exercising its right of derogation must "immediately inform"
the other state parties of the provisions of the ICCPR from which it has derogated,
and of "the reasons by which it was actuated." This provision "plainly calls for
notice to be dispatched almost simultaneously with the proclamation of the
emergency or the taking of derogating measures."[12] Uganda has never informed
the other state parties of any derogation of its ICCPR obligations, and has not yet
filed its initial country report on its compliance with ICCPR obligations which was
due to the Human Rights Committee, the U.N. body established under the ICCPR
to monitor its implementation, on September 20, 1996.

Freedom of Assembly

Like the right to freedom of association, the right to freedom of assembly is
protected under international law. Article 21 of the ICCPR states:

> The right of peaceful assembly shall be recognized. No restrictions may
> be placed on the exercise of this right other than those imposed in
> conformity with the law and which are necessary in a democratic
> society in the interests of national security or public safety, public order
> (*ordre public*), the protection of public health or morals or the
> protection of the rights and freedoms of others.[13]

Freedom of assembly is also recognized in the African Charter in Article 11, and
in Article 20 of the Universal Declaration which reads "Everyone has the right to
freedom of peaceful assembly and association."[14] According to one legal authority,
"The right to freedom of assembly [contained in the Universal Declaration] is

---

[11]Thomas Buergenthal, "State Obligations and Permissible Derogations," in Henkin
(ed.), *The International Bill of Rights*, p. 79.

[12]Buergenthal, "State Obligations and Permissible Derogations," p. 84.

[13]ICCPR, Art. 21.

[14]Universal Declaration of Human Rights, Article 20(1).

subject only to one condition, that it be exercised peacefully."[15] Peaceful assembly "refers exclusively to the conditions under which the assembly is held, i.e., 'without uproar, disturbance, or the use of arms.'"[16] This right includes the right of the individual to participate or not, and the right of groups or organizations to convoke an assembly or take part in it.[17] Peaceful assembly includes demonstrations in public places and meetings held indoors.[18]

Like the right to freedom of association, the right of peaceful assembly must be considered to have a political dimension: "the focus of freedom of assembly is clearly on its *democratic function* in the process of forming, expressing and implementing political opinions."[19] In order to be justified, restrictions on the right to freedom of assembly must be a) imposed in conformity with the law, b) serve one of the purposes listed in Article 21, and c) be necessary in a democratic society.

Political Rights: Article 25 of the International Covenant on Civil and Political Rights

Article 25 of the ICCPR provides for an important spectrum of political rights:

> Every citizen shall have the right and the opportunity, without any of the distinctions mentioned in Article 2 [forbidding discrimination] and without unreasonable restrictions:
> (a) To take part in the conduct of public affairs, directly or through freely chosen representatives;
> (b) To vote and to be elected at genuine periodic elections which shall be by universal and equal suffrage and shall be held by secret ballot, guaranteeing the free expression of the will of the electors;
> (c) To have access, on general terms of equality, to public service in his country.

---

[15]Partsch, "Freedom of Conscience and Expression, Political Freedoms," p. 233.

[16]Ibid., p. 231 (footnote omitted).

[17]Ibid., p. 233.

[18]Article 11, African Charter on Human and Peoples' Rights: "Every individual shall have the right to assemble freely with others. The exercise of this right shall be subject only to necessary restrictions provided for by law, in particular those enacted in the interest of national security, the safety, health, ethics and rights and freedoms of others."

[19]Nowak, *CCPR Commentary*, p. 370.

Some political rights are also recognized in article 21 of the Universal Declaration of Human Rights and article 13 of the African Charter.[20]

The U.N. Human Rights Committee, which monitors compliance with the ICCPR has elaborated on states' obligations in its General Comment 25 (57) on Article 25.[21] The committee elaborates on the need for free communication of information and ideas about public and political issues between citizens, candidates, and elected representatives. There must be a free press and other media able to comment without censorship or restraint. There must be freedom to engage in political activity individually or through political parties and other organizations, freedom to debate public affairs, to hold peaceful demonstrations and meetings, to criticize and oppose, to publish political material, to campaign for election, and to advertise political ideas. The Human Rights Committee closely ties the rights contained in article 25 to the rights of association, assembly, and free speech in its authoritative commentary:

> The right to freedom of association, including the right to form and join organizations and associations concerned with political and public affairs, is an essential adjunct to the rights protected by article 25. *Political parties and membership in parties play a significant role in the conduct of public affairs and the elections process.* States should ensure that, in their internal management, political parties respect the

---

[20]Article 21 of the Universal Declaration of Human Rights reads:
1. Everyone has the right to take part in the government of his country, directly or through freely chosen representatives.
2. Everyone has the right to equal access to public service in his country.
3. The will of the people shall be the basis of the authority of government; this will shall be expressed in periodic and genuine elections which shall be by universal and equal suffrage and shall be held by secret vote or by equivalent free voting procedure.

Article 13 of the African [Banjul] Charter on Human and Peoples' Rights reads:
1. Every citizen shall have the right to participate freely in the government of his country, either directly or through freely chosen representatives in accordance with the provisions of the law.
2. Every citizen shall have equal access to the public service of his country.
3. Every individual shall have the right of access to public property and services in strict equality of all persons before the law.
[21]General Comment No.25(57), U.N. Document CCPR/C/21/Rev.1/Add.7.

applicable provisions of article 25 in order to enable citizens to exercise rights thereunder.[22]

The Harare Commonwealth Declaration, adopted by Commonwealth Heads of Government (including Uganda) in 1991, echoes the obligations of states party to the ICCPR. Commonwealth states are committed, among other things, to respect "the individual's inalienable right to participate by means of free and democratic political processes in forming the society in which he or she lives."[23]

International Standards and the Regulation of Political Organizations

The internationally recognized right to freedom of association does not prohibit the regulation of political parties or other forms of political organizations. Indeed, most countries regulate political parties in order to ensure fairness in the political arena. However, regulations placed on political parties must meet the specific standards contained in the international covenants in order to be permissible. Most importantly, regulations on political parties cannot be so severe as to undermine the very content of the right to freedom of association. Because the right of political association is at the very core of the right to association, restrictions affecting political parties should be closely scrutinized to ensure that they do not undermine the core values of this important right.

A panel of thirty-one distinguished experts met in 1984 at Siracusa, Sicily, in order to adopt a uniform set of interpretations of the limitation clauses contained in the ICCPR, including the limitation clauses contained in article 22(2) of the ICCPR. The *Siracusa Principles on the Limitation and Derogation Provisions in the International Covenant on Civil and Political Rights* ("the Siracusa Principles") provides authoritative guidance to the meaning of the terms used in the limitation clauses. In addition to defining the different grounds for limitation of rights (see below), the Siracusa Principles provide some general interpretative guidelines for the justification of limitations of ICCPR rights. The following general principles are of greatest relevance to the interpretation of limitations on the rights of political parties:

- The scope of the limitation referred to in the covenant shall not be interpreted so as to jeopardize the essence of the right concerned.
- All limitations shall be interpreted strictly and in favor of the rights at issue.

---

[22]General Comment No.25(57), para 27 (emphasis added).

[23]Harare Commonwealth Declaration, issued at the Commonwealth Summit, Harare, October 20, 1991.

- Whenever a limitation is required in the terms of the covenant to be "necessary," this term implied that the limitation:

    (a) is based on one of the grounds justifying limitations recognized by the relevant article of the covenant;

    (b) responds to a pressing public or social need;

    (c) pursues a legitimate aim; and

    (d) is proportionate to that aim.

Any assessment of the necessity of a limitation shall be made on objective considerations.

- In applying a limitation, a state shall use no more restrictive means than are required for the achievement of the purpose of the limitation.[24]

The language of the right to freedom of association contained in article 22 of the ICCPR includes explicit guidelines which must be followed when placing limits on the right to freedom of association.[25] First, restrictions on freedom of association must be imposed by law, such as a parliamentary act. The restrictions must be *necessary in a democratic society* to advance one of the defined purposes in article 22(2), and this requirement has been interpreted to mean that restrictions must "be proportional and be oriented along the basic democratic values of pluralism, tolerance, broad-mindedness and peoples' sovereignty."[26] The Siracuse principles comment that "necessary in a democratic society" must be interpreted as imposing a further restriction on permissible limitations, requiring the state to demonstrate that the limitation does not impair the democratic functioning of society.[27]

---

[24]"The Siracusa Principles on the Limitation and Derogation Provisions in the International Covenant on Civil and Political Rights," *Human Rights Quarterly*, vol. 7, no. 1 (February 1985), principles 2, 3, 10, and 11.

[25] Article 22(2) of the ICCPR reads:

No restrictions may be placed on the exercise of this right other than those which are prescribed by law and which are necessary in a democratic society in the interest of national security or public safety, public order (*ordre public*), the protection of public health or morals or the protection of the rights and freedoms of others. This article shall not prevent the imposition of lawful restrictions on members of the armed forces and of the police in their exercise of this right.

[26] Nowak, *CCPR Commentary*, p. 394.

[27]Siracusa Principles 19-20.

The permissible grounds for the limitation of the right to freedom of association are exhaustively listed in article 22(2). Article 22(2) of the ICCPR envisions the following grounds for limitation:

- *National security*[28]
- *Public order*[29]
- *Public health*[30]
- *Public morals*[31]

---

[28]According to Siracusa Principles 29-32:
- National security may be invoked to justify measures limiting certain rights only when they are taken to protect the existence of the nation or its territorial integrity or political independence against force or threat of force;
- National security cannot be invoked as a reason for imposing limitations to prevent merely local or relatively isolated threats to law and order;
-National security cannot be used as a pretext for imposing vague or arbitrary limitations and may only be invoked when there exists adequate safeguards and effective remedies against abuse;
- The systematic violation of human rights undermines true national security and may jeopardize international peace and security. A state responsible for such violation shall not invoke national security as a justification for measures aimed at suppressing opposition to such violation or at perpetrating repressive practices against its population.
[29]Siracusa Principles 22-23:
- The expression "public order (*ordre public*)" as used in the Covenant may be defined as the sum of rules which ensure the functioning of society or the set of fundamental principles on which society is founded. Respect for human rights is part of public order (*ordre public*);
- Public order (*ordre public*) shall be interpreted in the context of the purpose of the particular human right which is limited on this ground
[30]Siracusa Principles 25-26:
- Public health may be invoked as a ground for limiting certain rights in order to allow a state to take measures dealing with a serious threat to the health of the population or individual members of the population. These measures must be specifically aimed at preventing disease or injury or providing care for the sick and injured;
-Due regard shall be had to the international health regulations of the World Health Organization.
[31]Siracusa Principles 27-28:
- Since public morality varies over time and from one culture to another, a state which invokes public morality as a ground for restricting human rights, while enjoying a certain margin of discretion, shall demonstrate that the limitation in question is essential to the maintenance of respect for fundamental values of the community.

•   *Protection of the rights and freedoms of others.*[32]

Democracy and Civil and Political Rights

Democracy is a contested term, defined in a multitude of ways by various commentators. Democracy has been defined variously as "a distinctive set of political institutions and practices, a particular body of rights, a social and economic order, a system that ensures desirable results, or a unique process for making collective and binding decisions."[33] However, as its Greek roots suggest, the essence of democracy is rule by the majority or popular sovereignty.[34] This view is reflected in article 21(3) of the Universal Declaration of Human Rights which states that "The will of the people shall be the basis of the authority of government."[35] The Council of Europe has clearly linked democracy to human rights, holding that democracy "means a pluralistic parliamentary democracy which, moreover, is characterised by respect for human rights and fundamental freedoms."[36] The 1993 World Conference on Human Rights also recognized the interdependence of human rights and democracy in its Vienna Declaration:

> Democracy, development and respect for human rights and fundamental
> freedoms are interdependent and mutually reinforcing. Democracy is
> based on the freely expressed will of the people to determine their own
> political, economic, social and cultural system and their full

---

- The margin of discretion left to states does not apply to the rule of non-discrimination as defined in the Covenant.

[32] According to Siracusa Principles 35-36:

- The scope of the rights and freedoms of others that may act as a limitation upon rights in the Covenant extends beyond the rights and freedoms recognized in the Covenant;

- When a conflict exists between a right recognized in the Covenant and one which is not, recognition and consideration should be given to the fact that the Covenant seeks to protect the most fundamental rights and freedoms. In this context especial weight should be afforded to rights not subject to limitation in the Covenants.

[33] Robert Dahl, *Democracy and Its Critics* (New Haven: Yale University Press, 1989), p. 5.

[34] The root meaning of the Greek term *demokratia*: *demos* translates as "people," while *kratia* translates as "rule" or "authority," thus leading to the concept of "rule by the people."

[35] Universal Declaration of Human Rights, article 21(3).

[36] Heinrich Klebes, "Human Rights and Parliamentary Democracy in the Parliamentary Assembly," in Franz Matscher and Herbert Petzold (eds.), *Protecting Human Rights: The European Dimension* (Köln: Carl Heymans, 1988).

participation in all aspects of their lives. In the context of the above, the promotion and protection of human rights and fundamental freedoms at the national and international levels should be universal and conducted without conditions attached. The international community should support the strengthening and promotion of democracy, development and human rights and fundamental freedoms in the entire world.[37]

Although an interpretation recognizing substantive political rights was opposed by the Soviet-bloc countries at the time of the adoption of the covenants and other human rights instruments, it is today's prevailing interpretation that the political rights contained in the ICCPR and the concept of government based on the will of the people contained in the Universal Declaration of Human Rights require a political system which is competitive and which allows for the actual existence of choices. The full realization of the concept of a government based on the will of the people requires that the electorate can actually change the government if a majority is dissatisfied with its policies.

The rights with a political dimension contained in the ICCPR—the article 25 political rights as well as the right to association, assembly, and speech—form the basis for a right to organized political opposition activity. Political parties have the right not only to formally and legally incorporate themselves under the right to freedom of association, but also to sponsor candidates for elections, hold peaceful political rallies, and freely express their opinions. Free and fair elections require a framework for the enjoyment of civil and political rights to be in place. This framework should include at a minimum:

1) the right of access to alternative sources of information, independent of the government;

2) freedom of opinion and expression;

3) freedom to organize in political parties and to vote and to be elected in genuine periodic elections.

These basic civil and political rights must be supported by the institutions necessary to enforce them, such as an army and police force which respect and enforce human rights. If violations occur, courts should hold government to account.

---

[37]World Conference on Human Rights, The Vienna Declaration and Programme of Action (Vienna, June 1993), paragraph 8.

Since independence, some African leaders have challenged the full implementation of political rights as a "western" concept of democracy inapplicable to the Third World. Many African countries became one party states after achieving independence, attempting to build party mobilizing governments in which "[p]articipation was open to all those who accepted the government's ideology and identified with its goals."[38] They attempted to create a national identity by limiting participation to one government sanctioned political party and aligned women's, youth, peasants, and workers' groups.[39] At the same time, African liberation movements often drew significant inspiration from the Universal Declaration of Human Rights and other bodies of human rights principles.

The one-party states of Africa shared certain characteristics. Most were headed by a charismatic leader who had broad executive powers, undermining the independence of other branches of government, the judiciary and the legislature. In many African one-party states, mass popular participation was used in a controlled fashion to give the government a semblance of legitimacy.[40]

Political opposition activities were often outlawed and in many cases severely suppressed. President Nyerere of Tanzania did not permit opposition to his ideology of *ujamaa* or African socialism, arguing that "if [ujamaa is] to form the basis on which society operates, then no advocacy of opposition to these principles can be allowed."[41] As in Uganda today, rival political parties were often restricted or outlawed on the grounds of being divisive or sectarian, or contrary to national unity:

> Another way to reduce opposition was to outlaw rival political organizations based on particularistic, sectarian, or ethnic interests. Ghana ... together with Guinea, paved the way for such actions by declaring local political parties illegal and contrary to national interests.

---

[38]Naomi Chazan et al., *Politics and Society in Contemporary Africa* (Boulder: Lynne Rienner Publishers, 1988), p. 166.

[39]Ibid.

[40]Michael Bratton and Nicolas van de Walle, *Democratic Experiments in Africa: Regime Transitions in Comparative Perspective* (Cambridge: Cambridge University Press, 1997), pp. 78-79, comment:

> Mass participation was orchestrated from above and channeled through symbolic rituals of endorsement for the personal ruler, his office holders and his policies. ... Despite these participatory rituals, the plebiscitary one party system was decidedly undemocratic because it precluded genuine political participation.

[41]Colin Legum and Geoffrey Mmari, *Mwalimu: The Influence of Nyerere* (Trenton: Africa World Press, 1995), p. 69.

In Kenya, Jomo Kenyatta hounded opposition leaders and accused them of fueling regional and separatist tendencies; in Sierra Leone, traditional institutions were manipulated; and in Guinea, chieftaincy was declared illegal. With alternate power constellations enfeebled, reconstructed opposition parties were on tenuous ground when they sought to mobilize support or criticize government actions.[42]

Most one party states in Africa ended in failure. President Nyerere recognized in 1990 that a party with a monopoly on power easily becomes complacent and stagnates.[43] The one-party state model was abandoned in Tanzania in 1992, and by 1994 most African countries had either adopted more representative political systems or were led by leaders who had successfully resisted or manipulated pressures to democratize, such as then-Zaire under President Mobutu. However, the one-party state model experimented with in Africa, and the severe restrictions it placed on political rights, has had a lasting impact on the political arena in those countries subjected to its restrictions. In many former African one-party states, democratic institutions continue to be extremely weak, at least partly due to the corrosive effects of decades of one party rule, military dictatorship, and colonial heritage.

---

[42]Chazon et al., *Politics and Society in Contemporary Africa*, p. 46.
[43]Legum and Mmari, *Mwalimu*, p. 74.

V. HISTORICAL BACKGROUND

Many current arguments advanced by Uganda's NRM government in favor of the movement government are based on its interpretation of Uganda's brutal post-colonial experience. As summarized in one recent account of Uganda's history:

> The dream of Ugandan independence quickly became a nightmare from which the country has yet to emerge. Understanding the dimensions of this tragedy requires an appreciation of the interrelationship between Uganda's ethnic diversity, the central government's increasing ineffectiveness, the emergence of the military as a political actor, and the proliferation of weak, brutal, and incompetent leaders.[44]

The Colonial Period

Like nearly all countries in Africa, Uganda's borders were determined by colonial powers with little regard for the ethnic composition of the country. Uganda was created out of several historical kingdoms in the south, the most powerful being the Buganda kingdom, and the less organized ethnic groups in the north. Tensions between the Nilotic-speaking northerners and the Bantu-speaking southerners have been a dominant theme in Uganda's history. Tensions along religious lines, mostly among Roman Catholics, Protestants, and Muslims have at times flared into violent confrontation and competion for political dominance.[45]

British colonial rule in Uganda was consolidated by the 1890 treaty with Buganda, closely followed by the 1894 declaration of a British protectorate over Uganda. British efforts to assert control over what became Uganda focused initially on the centrally located and well-organized Buganda kingdom. A 1900 agreement between the British and Buganda chiefs acknowledged British sovereignty and gave a privileged status to the Buganda kingdom, dividing Buganda land equally between the British and the Buganda chiefs, many of whom held the land in private ownership and leased plots to tenants under a system called

---

[44]Thomas P. Ofcansky, *Uganda: Tarnished Pearl of Africa* (Boulder: Westview Press 1996), p. 39.

[45]See generally, Holger Bernt Hansen and Michael Twaddle (eds.), *Religion and Politics in East Africa: The Period Since Independence* (London: James Currey, 1995). Some academics have argued that political parties exacerbated these ethnic and religious divides. See Dan M. Mudoola, *Religion, Ethnicity and Politics in Uganda* (Kampala: Fountain Publishers, 1996).

mailo tenure.[46] The British instituted a system of indirect governance in Uganda, often relying on Buganda proxies to conquer and administer other Ugandan kingdoms.[47] The Baganda—the people of the kingdom of Buganda—played a central role in colonial administration until independence, and through their close association with the colonial power, were able to obtain a privileged position in Ugandan society as reflected in the name of the colony.[48]

The preferential treatment accorded the Baganda contrasted sharply with British policy towards the Nilotic and Sudanic tribes of northern Uganda, who lacked the centralized structure of the Baganda and were thus considered more "backward." The northern region was not developed during the colonial period, and served mainly as a reservoir for cheap labor to be deployed in the south. Not wishing to further bolster the already disproportionate power of the Baganda, Britain recruited its soldiers mostly from the northern region: "Recruitment was reserved for Northerners and people from the East—who, it was argued, were naturally martial—lest the Baganda became too strong and colonial rule was endangered. The army became a despised profession, suitable only for uneducated people."[49] At the time of independence in 1962, the Ugandan army was predominantly northern, and the rapid expansion of the army during the first

---

[46]Ofcansky, *Uganda*, p. 22. On *mailo* land tenure, see generally W. Kisamba-Mugerwa, "Institutional Dimensions of Land Tenure Reform," in Holger Bernt Hansen and Michael Twaddle, *Changing Uganda: The Dilemmas of Structural Adjustment and Revolutionary Change* (London: James Currey, 1991), pp. 311-21.

[47]Indirect governance refers to the colonial practice of using local chiefs to extend colonial rule and the practice of using certain ethnic groups to assist in pacifying and ruling over others. Indirect governance through local intermediaries allowed the colonial powers to control the colony with a small number of expatriate officials.

[48]According to one authority:
Inevitably, Buganda became the hub of the economic activity of the protectorate: after all, Kampala and Entebbe, respectively its commercial and administrative capitals, were located in Buganda. . . . Nowhere was the disparity of development emphasised more than in education; it was the means by which southerners, especially Baganda, came to dominate the affairs of the country.
Phares Mutibwa, *Uganda Since Independence: A Story of Unfulfilled Hopes* (Trenton, N.J.: Africa World Press, 1992), pp. 8-9.

[49]Ibid., p. 6. See also Samwiri Lwanga-Lunyiigo, "The Colonial Roots of Internal Conflict," in Kumar Rupesinghe (ed.), *Conflict Resolution in Uganda* (Oslo: International Peace Research Institute, 1989); and Amii Omara-Otunnu, *Politics and the Military in Uganda* (London: Macmillan, 1987).

government of Milton Obote (1962-1971) continued to rely primarily on recruits from the northern regions of Acholi, Teso, Lango, and the West Nile.[50]

The legacy of these colonial policies continues to be felt in present day Uganda, and has played an important role in political developments since independence. The Independence Constitution of 1962 granted full federal status to the Buganda kingdom and semi-federal status to a number of other southern kingdoms (Ankole, Bunyoro, and Toro). The disposition of the 9,000 square miles of *mailo* land in Buganda remains a topic of significant controversy, as demonstrated by the 1998 debates about the proposed land bill which included threats of armed opposition by some Buganda leaders (discussed below). The tension between a developed center and underdeveloped north, northern dominance of the military, and inter-ethnic conflicts between different factions in the army, formed the basis for much of the instability that marked Uganda's post-independence experience.

Uganda's Independence and the First Obote Government

Uganda obtained independence in 1962 under a coalition government of Milton Obote's predominantly protestant Uganda People's Congress (UPC) and the Buganda traditionalist's political party *Kabaka Yekka* (KY, which translates as "The King Alone"). Milton Obote, a northerner, became prime minister and chose the Buganda's *Kabaka* (king) as his largely ceremonial president when Uganda became a republic in 1963. The ruling coalition soon broke up over disagreements about the "lost counties" issue—Bunyoro territory which was transferred to the Baganda by the British in reward for their loyalty—which Obote submitted to a referendum in November 1964.[51] The referendum led to a return of some of the disputed territory to the Bunyoro, and led to increased discontent with the Obote administration in Buganda.

In 1964, anti-Obote elements, led by UPC Secretary-General Ibingira, attempted to push Obote out of power by accusing Obote and Deputy Army Commander Idi Amin of involvement in a gold and ivory scandal. Obote responded to the attempted putsch by arresting the main plotters, suspending the 1962 Constitution, promoting Idi Amin to army chief of staff, and deposing the *Kabaka* from the presidency. In April 1966, Obote convened the national assembly

---

[50]E.A. Brett, "Neutralising the Use of Force in Uganda: The Role of the Military in Politics," *Journal of Modern African Studies*, vol. 33 no. 1 (1995), p. 135.
[51]The referendum allowed the residents of the lost counties to decide whether they wanted to remain part of the autonomous Buganda, return to Bunyoro district, or become an independent district.

to write a new republican constitution, entrenching a strong executive presidency and substantially reducing the powers of the traditional leaders. The new constitution led to increased tensions with the traditional Buganda legislature, the *lukiko*, which rejected the new constitution and the limitations it imposed on Buganda federal powers. Obote responded by declaring a state of emergency and ordering the army to attack and occupy the *Kabaka*'s palace in Mengo. The palace attack is estimated to have cost more than one hundred lives. *Kabaka* Mutesa II managed to escape to exile in London, where he later died.[52]

Over the next years, Obote consolidated his powers by introducing a new constitution in 1967 which abolished the four kingdoms and further strengthened executive powers. Following an assassination attempt on Obote in 1969, the UPC banned all opposition groups and effectively created a one party state.

Idi Amin's Reign of Terror

While Obote was preoccupied with consolidating his political grip on Uganda, Idi Amin was simultaneously establishing effective control over a significant part of the Ugandan armed forces. Ethnic tensions between different northern groups in the army soon developed:

> [F]rom the beginning of 1969, Obote had divided the army into two factions along ethnic lines. As President and the Chairman of the Defence Council, he relied on the Nilotic soldiers, largely from Acholi and Lango, while for his part Amin built his support on his fellow West Nilers, especially those who happened to be Sudanic people like himself.[53]

Tensions between Obote and Amin grew as Obote attempted to limit Amin's power base within the army, and Amin grew increasingly convinced that Obote was attempting to neutralize him. Just prior to leaving for Singapore in January 1971 to attend a summit conference of Commonwealth leaders, Obote asked Amin to account for 2.5 million pounds sterling spent by the army. With Obote away in Singapore, Amin responded by taking power on January 25, 1971.

Many Ugandans, especially those living in Buganda and other areas dissatisfied with Obote's increasingly oppresive government, initially welcomed

---

[52]On this chapter of Uganda's history, see I.K.K. Lukwago, *The Politics of National Integration in Uganda* (Nairobi: Coign Publications, 1982); and I.V. Satyamurthy, *The Political Development of Uganda (1900-1986)* (Aldershot: Gower, 1986).

[53]Mutibwa, *Uganda Since Independence*, pp. 8-9.

Amin's military coup. The release of many detainees and Amin's decision to allow *Kabaka* Mutesa II's body to return from England for burial were popular measures. The initial euphoria soon turned to horror as the true nature of Amin's government became clear. Amin soon ordered the army's Acholi and Langi elements, whom he considered rivals for power, to return to the barracks and had hundreds of officers and enlisted men killed.[54] Soon after, Amin created several new security organizations which reported directly to him, including the Public Safety Unit and the State Research Bureau:

> Along with the Military Police, these two organizations wreaked havoc on Uganda. By the end of Amin's first year in office, these security forces had killed approximately 10,000 Ugandans. Over the next few years, tens of thousands of Ugandans fell prey to Amin's henchmen, sought sanctuary in neighboring countries, or went into hiding in Uganda.[55]

A report by the New York City Bar Association's Committee on International Human Rights estimated the number of victims of Amin's reign of terror between 100,000 and 500,000.[56] Many prominent Ugandans lost their lives during Amin's reign of terror, including Chief Justice Benedicto Kiwanuka and Anglican archbishop Janani Luwuum.

In 1972, in an attempt to shore up domestic support, Amin ordered the expulsion of Uganda's 70,000 citizens of Asian origin and the expropriation of

---

[54]Robert Gersony, *The Anguish of Northern Uganda: Results of a Field-Based Assessment of the Civil Conflicts in Northern Uganda* (Kampala: U.S. Agency for International Development, August 1997), p. 7.

[55]Ofcansky, *Uganda*, p. 44.

[56]According to the report:

Within three months after he took power . . . Amin suspended all democratic rights, gave the army dictatorial powers of arrest and punishment, and set up a military tribunal to try political offenders. A period of terror administered by the Army (now dominated by Kakwa and Nubian ethnic groups from Amin's West Nile region) and the security services followed. It is estimated that between 100,000 and 500,000 Ugandans lost their lives or disappeared during Amin's eight-year rule. These included a large number of Langi and Acholi, the northern groups which had formed the backbone of the Obote government, as well as many Baganda intellectuals.

James J. Busuttil et al., "Uganda at the Crossroads—A Report on Current Human Rights Conditions," *The Record*, October 1991.

their extensive property holdings, including 5,655 firms, factories, and farms and U.S. $400 million in personal goods.[57] Amin sought closer ties with radical governments such as Libya, and accused Israel of subverting Uganda: in March 1972 Amin ordered all Israelis to leave Uganda. The Asian expulsion order, Amin's nationalization of British companies in 1973, and the failure to explain the death of Dora Bloch, a British woman killed by the Ugandan army in apparent retaliation for the Israeli raid on Entebbe to rescue hostages held by Palestinian terrorists, led to a break in relations between Uganda and Britain.

Amin finally overreached himself when he ordered the annexation of 1,800 square miles of Tanzanian territory known as the Kagera salient. President Nyerere of Tanzania, already a vocal critic of Amin's government, responded by ordering his troops—joined by various anti-Amin Ugandan militias under the rubric of the Uganda National Liberation Army (UNLA)—to invade Uganda and oust Amin. On April 10, 1979, Amin's government fell. Idi Amin is still alive, living in Saudi Arabia, and has never been called to account for the human rights abuses which took place during his rule.

The Second Obote Government and the "Bush War"

Several short-lived civilian administrations followed the overthrow of the Amin government, culminating in a return to power by Obote in a disputed election in 1980. The sixty-eight-day Lule government, headed by former Makerere University vice chancellor and chairperson of the UNLA's political arm Yusef Lule, soon faltered because of Lule's perceived pro-Buganda slant and tensions between the UNLA's military and political wings.[58]

The UNLA ousted Yusef Lule and installed Godfrey Binaisa, the attorney general during Obote's first government, as president. Infighting within the UNLA prevented Binaisa from restoring stability in Uganda. In August 1979, Binaisa's government imposed a ban on political parties, believing that with such a ban Uganda would avoid "the politics of religion, sectarianism, rivalry and hatred, and be able to work for and even achieve the politics of consensus"[59]—an argument similar to the one made by President Museveni today. Pro-Obote forces within the military structures of the UNLA removed Binaisa from power on May 13, 1980,

---

[57]Ofcansky, *Uganda*, p. 44.

[58]Two years later, Lule would join his Uganda Freedom Fighters (UFF) with Museveni's Popular Resistance Army (PRA) to form the National Resistance Army (NRA) which ultimately took power in 1986, although Lule himself would die in exile in January 1985.

[59]Mutibwa, *Uganda Since Independence*, p. 134.

placing Binaisa under house arrest and scheduling an election for December 10, 1980.

The election of December 1980 proved to be a watershed event in Uganda's political history. Four parties—Obote's UPC, the predominantly Catholic Democratic Party (DP), the Uganda Patriotic Movement (UPM) of Yoweri Museveni, and the Buganda-dominated Conservative Party (CP)—took part in the elections. The election results gave the victory to Obote's UPC, and Obote returned to head Uganda for a second time. However, most international observers as well as the DP and UPM accused the pro-Obote military commission of rigging the election. The rigged elections may have stolen victory from the Democratic Party, but Museveni's UPM was only a minor player at the time of the elections and won only a single seat. Museveni himself was narrowly defeated in his Mbarara home district by a DP candidate.

Museveni has stated that these rigged elections and the corrupt and military-dominated system which returned Obote to power caused him to form the National Resistance Army (NRA) and wage a guerrilla war, with the aim not only of obtaining power but of causing a radical change in Uganda's system of governance. Museveni argued that his call to arms was a legitimate response to undemocratic practices: "Once again, a minority, unpopular clique was imposed on the people of Uganda, leaving them with no option but to take up arms in defense of their democratic rights."[60]

Museveni perceived his struggle against Obote as more than a struggle for power, describing it as a struggle to free Uganda from the political manipulations of elitist and nonrepresentative political parties and to create a more democratic and representative system of governance. The NRM's ten-point program blamed Uganda's woes on political manipulation, and urged the elimination of all forms of sectarianism (defined loosely as the ethnic, religious, regional and other divisions which according to the NRM have had a negative impact on political life in Uganda).

The period of civil war which followed was characterized by a wanton disregard for human rights by government troops and a massive loss of human lives, especially in the Buganda "Luwero triangle," the area of central Uganda near the capital Kampala:

---

[60]Yoweri Museveni, "Theoretical Justification of NRM Struggle," in *Mission to Freedom: Uganda Resistance News 1981-85* (Kampala: Directorate of Information and Mass Mobilization, NRM Secretariat, 1990), p. 3.

This period was characterized by military excesses against civilians which are believed to have exceeded the brutality of the Amin era. The worst assaults on civilians took place in an area of Buganda known as the Luwero triangle formed by roads leading north and northwest out of Kampala. By 1984, the U.S. State Department estimated that between 100,000 and 200,000 civilians were slaughtered in the Luwero triangle by the Obote regime, and by 1985, the number was believed to be far higher.[61]

Despite the repressive measures of the UNLA, the NRA/M continued to make significant progress in its guerrilla campaign against the Obote government. The strong anti-Obote sentiments in Buganda, where the bad memories of Obote's first government remained strong, ensured NRA/M support in the region. Other rebel groups, including the pro-Amin Uganda National Army (UNA) and the west-nile based Uganda National Rescue Front (UNRF), prevented the UNLA from focusing its resources against the NRA/M. In May 1985, interethnic tensions between Acholi and Langi (two neighboring northern ethnic groups) UNLA troops led Brigadier Basilio Okello and General Tito Lutwa Okello (unrelated Acholis) to depose Obote (a Langi) in a coup. Milton Obote currently lives in Zambia, and was never called to account for the human rights abuses committed during his rule.

The Okello government seized power on a platform of national reconciliation, urging all political parties and insurgent groups to join the new government. Although many insurgent groups joined the Okellos, the NRA/M refused to join partly because Museveni was dissatisfied with the number of seats on the ruling Military Council which were offered to the NRA/M. Between August and December 1985, the Okellos and the NRA/M engaged in talks in Nairobi, which

---

[61]Busuttil et al., "Uganda at the Crossroads—A Report on Current Human Rights Conditions." See also Ofcansky, *Uganda*, p. 54:

In January 1983, Obote launched "Operation Bonanza" in [the Luwero triangle], during which UNLA troops destroyed small towns, villages, and farms and killed or displaced hundreds of thousands of civilians. The carnage eventually attracted the world's attention, and several governments and humanitarian organizations condemned the Obote regime. According to Amnesty International, there were reports of at least thirty-six mass grave sites in the Luwero triangle. The Banyarwanda community, much of which had supported Amin, lost 45,000 to 60,000 people. After the war ended in 1986, the International Committee of the Red Cross claimed that at least 300,000 people had died in the Luwero triangle and that officials had failed to account for half to a third of the region's population.

ended in the Nairobi peace accord between Museveni and the Okello government.[62] However, the Nairobi peace accord was never implemented and Museveni continued his guerilla campaign against the Okello government. On the 26th of January 1986, Museveni's NRA/M defeated the Okello government and took Kampala, effectively establishing itself as the government of Uganda.

The Early NRM Period: Administrative Bans and Military Control

Almost immediately upon taking power, President Museveni announced that political party activity would be suspended during the transition period, which he pledged would not last more than four years. This ban on political activity was formalized by the first official act of the NRM government, Legal Notice No. 1 of 1986, which established the unelected National Resistance Council (NRC) to govern during the interim period. Many political forces in Uganda, including the Democratic Party, initially accepted the restrictions on political parties, assuming them to be an interim arrangement, and accepted the NRM's invitation to form a broad coalition government. Paul Ssemogerere, president of the DP, told Human Rights Watch:

> Despite our opposition to armed solutions, we accepted the moral cause of Museveni. When he eventually captured power, there was lots of sympathy for him. He fought a good cause and promised the necessary constitutional reforms to restore democracy. When he wanted us to join him, we accepted to work with him as an interim arrangement. So the Democratic Party's National Executive Committee accepted to work with Museveni.[63]

Although dominated by the NRM/A representatives, Museveni's coalition government initially included members of the DP, the UPC, the pro-Amin Uganda National Rescue Front (UNRF), as well as two Buganda-based rebel groups, the

---

[62]Museveni's own writings suggest that the NRA/M never seriously considered that the adversaries would abide by the terms of the peace agreement: "[E]ven while we signed the agreement...we knew that the provisions would not work as long as the Okellos were motivated by power and nobody was fully in control of the army. The UNLA's massacre of civilians continued even after we had signed the peace accord and we knew we had no option but to continue with the war against them." Museveni, *Sowing the Mustard Seed*, p. 169.

[63]Human Rights Watch interview with Paul Ssemogerere, President, Democratic Party, Mengo, May 7, 1998.

Federal Democratic Movement of Uganda (FEDEMU) and the Uganda Freedom Movement/Army (UFM/A).[64] However, the coalition grew narrower over time: "All these groups eventually withdrew from the coalition, citing the government's complicity in human rights violations, official corruption, continuing instability in northern and eastern Uganda, the creation of tribal animosities, and communist and Libyan infiltration of Uganda."[65] Despite promises in 1986 that the NRC would hold office for a period "not exceeding four years," Museveni extended the interim period for another five year period in 1989, claiming that continued insurgency in the country had prevented the NRM administration from reaching its original objectives in the initial four year period.[66] The membership of the NRC was expanded through an indirect election in 1989.

During the first years of the NRM administration, the government faced armed opposition in the north, east, and southwest. During the course of its anti-insurgency operations, the NRA detained thousands of civilians suspected of supporting the rebels, holding them unlawfully without charges at military barracks as "lodgers." In July 1989, sixty-nine persons in NRA custody died at Mukuru, Soroti district, after suffocating in a locked train compartment. Opponents and critics of the NRM government faced harassment and arrest by the government. Lance Seera Muwanga, secretary-general of the Uganda Human Rights Activists group, at the time the only human rights NGO in Uganda, was arrested in February 1987 after giving an interview to the *Africa Concord* magazine in which he criticized the NRM's human rights record. He was released in March 1988, and went into exile to Sweden soon thereafter. Cecilia Ogwal, a leading member of the UPC, gave Human Rights Watch details of ten incidents in which she was arrested and briefly detained but never charged between 1991 and 1993, mostly after attempts to hold meetings with fellow UPC leaders.[67]

The tactics used to repress political activity during the period of the administrative ban on political activities revealed a readiness to resort to strong shows of force, and had a lasting chilling effect on the willingness of Ugandans to challenge restrictions on political activity which remain in effect today. Many of the persons interviewed by Human Rights Watch described one particularly well known incident in Kampala in May 1993. The Democratic Party (DP) Mobilizers,

---

[64]Ofcansky, *Uganda*, pp. 53, 60.

[65]Ibid., p. 60.

[66]Major Ondoga ori Amaza, *Museveni's Long March: From Guerrilla to Statesman* (Kampala: Fountain Publishers, 1998), pp. 155-56.

[67]Human Rights Watch interview with Cecilia Ogwal, Chairperson, Interim Executive Committee of the UPC, Kampala, April 13, 1998.

an offshoot of the Democratic Party under the leadership of Michael Kaggwa, attempted to hold a public rally in Kampala to openly challenge the ban on political activity. According to international press reports, Museveni responded to the planned rally by stating in parliament that those who attended the rally would be killed: "I have told the police to stop political gatherings using force. Tell your supporters that they will be killed if they attend political rallies."[68] Police effectively sealed off the city and army helicopters were brought in to intimidate party supporters.[69] DP-Mobilizer officials called off the planned rally to prevent bloodshed.

A similar rally organized by the DP-Mobilizers in November 1993 was called off after hundreds of riot police wielding batons and teargas canisters sealed off the proposed venue of the rally in Kampala.[70]

The Odoki Commission

The Uganda Constitutional Commission, known popularly as the Odoki Commission after its chairperson Justice Ben Odoki, was appointed in March 1989 to draft a new constitution for Uganda. Dean of Makerere Law School Joe Oloka-Onyango is among those who has questioned the make-up of the Odoki Commission, claiming that "almost to a person, it comprised strong adherents of the Movement system, incorporating therein both the Political Commissar of the NRM as well as his counterpart in the NRA."[71] The Odoki Commission conducted an impressive campaign to reach out to the Ugandan public and get their views on a new constitutional order, conducting seminars in all 870 subcounties of Uganda and collecting a total of more than 25,000 submissions, including over 800 submissions from religious, political, and other civil society groups.[72]

The Odoki Commission's final report, which included a proposed outline for the constitution, essentially adopted the restrictive political party system which currently operates in Uganda, claiming that this is what the population wanted.

---

[68]"Uganda's Museveni clamps down on political rally," Agence France Presse, May 8, 1993.

[69]Ibid.

[70]"Police Stop Opposition Rally in Kampala," Agence France Presse, November 13, 1993.

[71]Joe Oloka-Onyango, "Governance, State Structures and Constitutionalism in Contemporary Uganda," (Kampala: Centre for Basic Research, May 1998), p. 21.

[72]John M. Waliggo, "Constitution-making and the politics of democratisation in Uganda," in Holger Bernt Hansen and Michael Twaddle, *From Chaos to Order: The Politics of Constitution-Making in Uganda* (Kampala: Fountain Publishers, 1995), pp. 27-28.

Recognizing that the question of Uganda's future political system was "one of the most controversial at all levels of society," the Odoki Commission suggested that the one party option should be rejected but that Ugandans should be allowed to choose through periodic referendums whether they would like to be governed through the movement system or the multiparty system. The Odoki Commission's recommendations also set out a number of principles which should guide the movement, as well as a set of guiding principles for political parties. The detailed proposals of the Odoki Commission largely set the framework for the debates that followed in the constituent assembly.

The Constituent Assembly and the Making of the Constitution

Many of the debates which ultimately led to today's legal restrictions on civil and political rights took place in the Constituent Assembly in 1994-95. The original statute of the Odoki Commission envisioned a situation wherein the last stage of constitutional reform would be "the discussion and adoption of the draft constitution by a Constituent Assembly consisting of the National Resistance Council, the Army Council and other delegates."[73] However, in what has been described as "a rare democratic sentiment from a military source in Africa," the commander of the National Resistance Army, Major General Mugisha Muntu, chastised the members of the NRC for "fearing to face the electorate," and called for a renewed mandate from the people prior to the adoption of the constitution.[74]

The Constituent Assembly Election Act of 1993 provided the first opportunity for the NRM government to translate its administrative ban on political party activity into a legal ban. The election rules provided that candidates would "stand and be voted for...upon personal merit," and that any candidate who used or attempted to use any political party, tribal or religious affiliations or other "sectarian" grounds for purposes of the election would be disqualified.[75] Candidates were only allowed to campaign at rallies or meetings organized by the government, and no other "public rallies and any form of public demonstration in support of or against any candidate" were allowed.[76]

Despite the severe restrictions on political party activity, a significant number of opposition politicians decided to participate in the constituent assembly elections of March 1994. The decision by a UPC faction led by Cecilia Ogwal to participate

---

[73]Amaza, *Museveni's Long March*, p. 179.

[74]James Katorobo, "Electoral Choices in the Constituent Assembly elections of March 1994," in Hansen and Twaddle, *From Chaos to Order*, p. 119.

[75]Constituent Assembly Election Rules, Rule 11.

[76]Ibid., Rule 12.

in the elections led to an as yet unresolved split with their exiled leader Milton Obote, who advocated a complete rejection of the constitution-making exercise.[77] Despite a secret ballot and a universal franchise, the election restrictions put the political opposition at a disadvantage. However, many opposition politicians managed to be elected to the constituent assembly, although an exact count is difficult to reach because candidates could not state their party affiliation.[78]

As was expected, the issue of the future political system was one of the most controversial issues in the constituent assembly, together with the debates on Buganda's proposals for a decentralized federal system and the hotly debated issue of land reform. Considerable confusion ensued when high-ranking NRA officials, including Lieutenant Colonel Serwanga Lwanga, chief political commissar for the NRA, and Major General David Tinyefuza, an influential and high-ranking NRA delegate, put forth proposals for a rapid return to multiparty politics. Lwanga argued that the Odoki Commission was not representative of the views of all Ugandans, and suggested that many Ugandans might have changed their minds about supporting the NRM since being asked about the system by the Odoki Commission almost five years prior.[79] Major General Tinyefuza was more direct in his criticism of the proposed five-year extension of the movement system prior to the referendum:

> NRM has been in power for ten years. It did influence events even between 1981 to 1985. That makes it fifteen years. It is almost immoral to want another free extension of five years to make it twenty.[80]

The NRM responded by organizing a movement caucus to push through its views and to force adherence to its positions. Major General Tinyefuza was forced by the NRA's high command to make a humiliating apology, retracting his comments and

---

[77]After the participation by the Ogwal faction in the 1996 presidential and parliamentary elections, the UPC split into the Interim Executive Committee (IEC) faction headed by Cecilia Ogwal and the pro-Obote Presidential Policy Commission (PPC).

[78]Cecilia Ogwal of the UPC/IEC claims that 66 of the 214 elected seats were filled by opposition candidates, representing nearly one-third of the elected representatives. The multipartyists (i.e. those advocating an immediate return to a pluralist political system) formed the National Caucus for Democracy (NCD) in the assembly, ultimately walking out when it became clear that the NRM caucus would not negotiate over Uganda's future political system.

[79]Lieutenant Colonel Serwanga Lwanga, "Towards Stable and Orderly Governance" (dated May 19, 1995).

[80]Amaza, *Museveni's Long March*, p. 203.

promising "henceforth before expressing any opinion on any constitutional or political matter, I shall seek the guidance and authority of the appropriate organs of the army."[81] Ultimately the constituent assembly adopted a constitution on September 22, 1995, which placed severe restrictions on political party activity (see below).

---

[81]Oloka-Onyango, "Governance, State Structures and Constitutionalism in Contemporary Uganda," p. 16.

VI. THE MOVEMENT SYSTEM AND POLITICAL FREEDOMS IN UGANDA

Towards a Human Rights Culture in Uganda

The government of President Museveni has taken important steps towards establishing a human rights culture in Uganda, and marked a clear break with the abusive dictatorships which preceeded it. The widespread atrocities committed during the time of Idi Amin and Obote represent a traumatic past which Uganda wishes to avoid repeating, and some of the institutional reforms put into place by the NRM administration have indeed fostered a more accountable and representative government. Some newly created institutions, such as the Uganda Human Rights Commission, have played an important role in fostering a viable human rights culture in Uganda. The general human rights climate in Uganda has improved significantly because of these institutional changes introduced by the NRM administration.

The general improvement in the human rights record of Uganda, however, has been cited to distract attention from Uganda's record on freedoms with a political content, such as the rights to freedom of expression, association, and assembly. According to Justice Odoki, "I think that there is a great improvement in the general human rights situation in Uganda. You no longer see restrictions on basic freedoms and a state of anarchy in this country. But we underplay political freedoms in light of these advances."[82]

Commission of Inquiry into Human Rights Violations

In May 1986, soon after coming to power, the NRM established a commission of inquiry into human rights violations, charged with investigating the human rights record of all governments since independence until the seizure of power by the NRM. Although the commission's work was often hampered by a lack of funding and limitations in its mandate, it held extensive hearings throughout Uganda and significantly raised the level of rights awareness within the general population. Despite serious financial problems, the commission ultimately produced a final report of about 700 pages, in addition to a fifteen-volume verbatem record and a summary booklet for popular dissemination. The commission's report provided an analysis of the extent and causes of Uganda's past human rights woes, and offered detailed recommendations to the government about how to build a human rights culture. Among its chief recommendations were the appropriate punishment

---

[82]Human Rights Watch interview with Justice Odoki, Chair, Constitutional Commission, Kampala, April 4, 1998.

of human rights violators, the inclusion of human rights education in the general curriculum and in the training of the army and security forces, and the establishment of a permanent human rights commission.[83]

Uganda Human Rights Commission (HRC)

The proposal for a permanent human rights commission was amplified by the Odoki Constitutional Commission, which recommended the establishment of such a body in its final report, defining the proposed functions and powers in significant detail.[84] These proposals were ultimately adopted in the 1995 constitution,[85] and implemented through the Uganda Human Rights Commission Act of 1997.[86] The HRC started functioning in November 1996, when its chairperson Margaret Sekaggya and seven members were appointed by President Museveni.

The HRC has used its broad mandate and powers to become an effective and respected leader on human rights issues. Its commissioners have investigated a wide variety of human rights abuses, and have not shied away from issuing strongly worded condemnations of abusive practices by government officials, including the security forces.

The commission has undertaken detailed investigations into prison conditions throughout the country, visiting at least eighteen police stations and twenty-four local and central prisons and conducting workshops to improve prison conditions in Uganda. In June 1998, the human rights commission criticized a spate of arrests of about eighty Moslems, branding the conduct of the police and security agencies as illegal and demanding the immediate release of the detainees. A statement by the commission was unambigious: "The commission wishes to point out that whereas it does not condone criminal activities, the practise of detaining suspects in ungazetted places is unconstitutional and cannot in any way be legally justified under our law."[87] Similar strong statements were issued in regard to other human rights problems identified by the commission. In November 1998, it conducted its first public hearings into individual complaints, looking into allegations of human

---

[83]Commission of Inquiry into Violations of Human Rights, *Final Report* (Entebbe: UPPC, 1993).

[84]Uganda Constitutional Commission, *Report of the Uganda Constitutional Commission* (Entebbe: UPPC, 1993), pp. 185-88.

[85]Uganda Constitution (1995), Arts 51-58.

[86]Uganda Human Rights Commission Act (1997).

[87]"Uganda Rights Commission Demands Release of Detained Moslems," Agence France Presse, June 4, 1998.

rights abuses against senior police officers, UPDF members, and in one case a government minister.

The human rights commission's first annual report, on its 1997 work, was released in July 1998. The detailed seventy-page report discusses a wide variety of human rights violations, and does not shy away from identifying government culprits, including security officials. The HRC assisted Human Rights Watch in some of its investigations, providing information upon request. Ugandan NGOs in general were supportive of the HRC, although some activists told Human Rights Watch that they were concerned about a government body monopolizing the human rights field, and wished that the HRC would define a more limited mandate.

The work of the HRC continues to be stymied by a lack of adequate funding and, on many occasions, uncooperative government officials; the recommendations of the HRC are often ignored by government officials. Nonetheless, the HRC has shown a positive commitment to the full implementation of its mandate, and is likely to play an important role in improving Uganda's human rights record in the future.

Unfortunately, the commission has not directly addressed the issue of the movement system and violations of civil and political rights in Uganda to any significant degree, and has not issued any statements on these abuses. When Human Rights Watch discussed this issue with commissioners, it was clear that there was some division within the HRC on the issue of such violations, and that the majority of the commissioners prefered to remain silent on the issue. In early 1999, the Free Movement presented a petition to the HRC asking it to hold hearings into violations of civil and political rights associated with the movement system. Increasing public pressure could lead the HRC to take a closer look at such abuses.

The HRC is not the only body responsible for addressing human rights abuses in Uganda. The inspector general of government (IGG), the director for public prosecutions, and the Ugandan judiciary also contribute in obvious ways to the efforts to build a human rights culture in Uganda. In addition, the government has established human rights desks within the office of the president, the UPDF, and other bodies.

The Role of Parliament

The present Ugandan parliament was elected in 1996 under the "movement" system, which barred political parties from fielding and supporting candidates. Despite the severe restrictions placed on members of political parties, some opposition politicians decided to contest the elections in their personal capacity and were succesfully elected. The parliament thus includes a significant number of opposition politicians closely associated with political parties. Groups such as the Acholi parliamentary group, representing parliamentarians from Gulu and Kitgum districts, are examples of organized groups within parliament often at odds with government policies. The ability of such critical politicians to be elected and to then form groups to operate in parliament demonstrates that the government is willing to tolerate some organized opposition to controversial government policies.

The Ugandan parliament has become a vocal and progressive institution, and its actions in criticizing government corruption and abuse of office suggest a significant amount of independence from the executive branch. The parliament has been especially vocal in its investigation of official government corruption, its hearings leading to the resignations of two government ministers as well as Major General Salim Saleh, brother of President Museveni and formerly "overseer" of the UPDF. However, a majority of pro-movement parliamentarians has meant that reforming or ending the movement system are effectively out of reach of parliament.

The Decentralization Process

Under prior governments, civilians played only a minor role in politics, as politics was dominated by a small elite segment. In accordance with the 1995 constitution, Uganda has embarked on an ambitious program of government decentralization which aims to increase the role civilians play at all levels of government. In the process of decentralization, local governments are assuming some control over local taxation and development funds, an important mechanism of empowerment. The 1997 Local Government Act, which refines the five-level council system originally established (as "Resistance Councils") when the NRM came to power, is the centerpiece of this ongoing process of decentralization.[88] Human Rights Watch was present during local elections (conducted under the "movement" system") in Kampala and Kasese during April 1998, and the level of local participation in these elections was impressive. The council system allows significant civilian participation in the conduct of local government, although the impact of these local structures on national executive policies appears rather minimal. Despite their importance to local participation, these structures of local government do not present a counterweight to the continued dominance of the Ugandan executive in setting policy.

---

[88]For a general overview of the process of decentralization in Uganda, see Apolo Nsibambi (ed.), *Decentralisation and Civil Society in Uganda: The Quest for Good Governance* (Kampala: Fountain Publishers, 1998).

One of the important impacts of the political reforms implemented by the NRM administration has been the empowerment of women, a traditionally marginalized sector of society, at all levels of government. The administration has put into action strong affirmative action programs which aim to raise the level of participation of women in government, and women are represented in significant numbers at both the local and national level. Private initiatives such as those carried out by the Forum for Women in Democracy (FOWODE) undertake programs to prepare women to aspire for political leadership. President Museveni has shown a strong commitment to the empowerment of women in Uganda, often appointing women to important positions of leadership such as the position of vice president and chairperson of the human rights commission. Some women leaders interviewed by Human Rights Watch, however, expressed concern that President Museveni expected women leaders to be loyal to the "movement" system in return for the empowerment measures undertaken by the government.

Museveni's Theory of the No-Party State

The political restrictions in place in Uganda are based on the position, advocated by President Museveni and his National Resistance Movement, that Uganda's past political problems were mainly due to the ravages caused by divisive "sectarian politics." To remedy this, Museveni and the NRM advocate a "movement" or "no-party" political system in Uganda.

Museveni posits the "movement" or "no-party" system of government as an alternative to a multiparty system, and the necessary antidote to the perceived poisonous sectarianism of the political parties in Uganda. Instead of political parties which were viewed as divisive, Museveni introduced the idea of a "no-party" system, one supposedly all-inclusive movement in which individual candidates would run for elections based on their personal merit. A pyramid of five levels of councils, from the village to the national level, is designed to ensure grassroots participation at all levels of society. The Odoki Constitutional Commission attempted to define the movement system as follows:

> The movement political system is a unique initiative introduced in Uganda by the NRM administration since January 1986. It is based on democratically elected resistance councils from the village level to the National Resistance Council (Parliament). It is founded on participatory democracy which enables every person to participate in his or her own governance at all levels of government. ... It is all-embracing in its approach and vision. It has no manifesto of its own, apart from the commonly agreed upon programme. It does not recruit members, since

all people in Uganda are presumed to be members of the village resistance councils. At all times it aims to give expression to the people's sovereignty. During elections people vote for candidates based on their own merit and not on the basis of their party affiliation.[89]

Museveni has also argued that it is the movement system which is responsible for the achievements of his government: "It amuses me that we are complimented for the sustained economic growth which we have achieved in these last 12 years, for the way we have generally turned the country around from the mess we found it in. But at the same time our friends who pay us those compliments don't seem to realize that it is the political system which we established that has contributed to the advances made in the socioeconomic field. The two cannot really be divorced."[90]

The movement system has continued to evolve in often contradictory directions, and President Museveni has never clearly defined the movement system other than in terms of the dangers of "sectarianism" which it aims to prevent. The constant refrain during Museveni's 1996 presidential campaign was that a vote for his opponents would cause a return to the past, that former dictator Milton Obote was waiting in Zambia to return to power if Museveni was defeated. One of Museveni's presidential election posters featured a picture of skulls and bones beside a mass grave in Luwero, with the caption: "Don't forget the past. Over one million Ugandans, our brothers, sisters, family and friends, lost their lives. YOUR VOTE COULD BRING IT BACK"; another campaign advertisement stated bluntly, "A vote for Ssemogerere is a vote for Obote."[91]

According to President Museveni, most societies in sub-Saharan Africa are still in a pre-industrial stage, and have not yet developed the "economic class differentiation" which he argues forms the basis for the diverse political parties found in industrial nations.[92] Similarly, Museveni's and the NRM's views on the political maturity of the peasants who form the majority of the population are unflattering: Minister of State for Political Affairs Mbabazi told Human Rights

---

[89]Uganda Constitutional Commission, *Report of the Uganda Constitutional Commission: Analysis and Recommendations*, p. 197.

[90]"Speech by Ugandan President Yoweri Museveni in Kampala—Live," Kampala Radio Uganda Network, January 27, 1998.

[91]Chris McGreal, "Dark Past Haunts Ugandan Election," *Weekly Mail and Guardian* (South Africa), May 10, 1996.

[92]Museveni, *Sowing the Mustard Seed*, p. 187. See also, "Museveni Opposes Multi-Party System," Pan African News Agency, July 25, 1997.

Watch that "a peasant's conception of Uganda does not go beyond his village,"[93] echoing Museveni's view that "the hill is the outer limit of [a peasant's] horizon."[94] Using a pseudo-Marxist model, Museveni argues that because people in peasant societies lack a class identity, they are prone to ethnic and religious polarization, easily exploited by politicians who are "messengers of perpetual backwardness":

> Societies at this stage of development tend to have vertical polarisations based mainly on tribe and ethnicity.... This means that people support someone who belongs to their group, not because he puts forward the right policies. That delays the process of discovery of the truth and by the time the people wake up to the situation, many things have gone wrong or have passed us by.[95]

Such broad generalizations about the political consciousness of Ugandans ignore the fact that many Ugandans have looked beyond their own ethnic affiliations in recent elections. During the 1996 presidential elections, Paul Ssemogerere, the Baganda leader of the Democratic Party, found his most substantial support not in his home region but in northern Uganda, in large part because many northerners identified with his commitment to bring peace to the region.

Museveni and the NRM present political parties as the primary culprits for Uganda's past turmoil, and as a danger to Uganda's future peace and stability. These are typical comments made by President Museveni during the twelfth anniversary celebrations of the NRA's military victory:

> The political parties we had in Uganda, and the ones we still have—I hear them still saying they are organizing—are definitely organized along those lines, lines of tribes, lines of religion.... Well, we had elections recently in one of the East African countries [Kenya], and we should look at the results to see what multipartyism means in some of these situations.... In order to minimize the primordial political fault

---

[93]Human Rights Watch interview with Amama Mbabazi, Minister of State for Political Affairs, Kampala, May 5, 98.

[94]Quoted in Nelson Kasfir, "'No-Party Democracy' in Uganda," *Journal of Democracy*, April 1998, p. 60.

[95]Ibid., p. 187.

lines, which almost succeeded in destroying this country, we thought of another way to organize politics in our country.[96]

The view of the NRM that political parties were largely responsible for Uganda's post-independence woes finds strong resonance in the Ugandan population. Ugandans suffered greatly under the abusive governments of Idi Amin and Milton Obote, and the wish to avoid a return to such a period of abuse is almost universal. In the past, the leadership of some political parties such as the UPC have at times undermined democracy, quickly outlawing all other political parties after they gained power and triggering destructive civil wars around competition for political dominance. But while the fear of a return to the turmoil of the past is a legitimate concern for many Ugandans, it is also used by the current Ugandan government to justify present restrictions. Father Larry Kanyike, chaplain at Kampala's Makerere University, said that the current Ugandan government evoked the abusive regimes of Idi Amin and Milton Obote to validate itself: "Our leaders have taken advantage of this situation and, instead of giving the people what is rightfully theirs, they use the fears of the past as the determinant to promote legitimacy."[97]

The idea that political parties are "sectarian" is in many ways a self-fulfilling prophecy under the NRM's movement system. "Sectarianism" has become a broad concept encompassing any kind of activity perceived as divisive of national unity. Since the NRM defines itself as a movement which encompasses the whole nation—and to which all Ugandans are compelled to belong—it is difficult to escape the label of sectarianism when engaging in any political activity opposed to the NRM.

It is unclear whether the "no-party system" has had a diminishing effect on lowering the regional and ethnic divisions in Uganda. Most of the opposition politicians interviewed by Human Rights Watch viewed the NRM as a narrowly based political group from southwestern Uganda. The increasing marginalization of the north certainly has affected the popularity of the NRM administration in that region, as demonstrated by the low number of votes received there by Museveni during the 1996 presidential elections. Professor Nelson Kasfir among others has claimed that regional tensions have increased since 1986:

---

[96] "Speech by Ugandan President Yoweri Museveni in Kampala—Live," Kampala Radio Uganda Network.

[97] "Uganda Under Pressure to Embrace More Democracy," Reuters, Kampala, January 15, 1999.

Regional splits have deepened since the NRM came to power. Most of the top leadership of the NRM comes from the west, particularly from the former political unit of Ankole. Devastating civil wars have been fought in parts of the east and the north. The perception of the NRM as a 'southern' government, and the wars it has fought against the remnants of the armies of its former enemies, have reinforced regional cleavages.[98]

Despite his unconditional support for the movement system, President Museveni has on occasion suggested that the movement system may ultimately be a transitional system: "what is crucial for Uganda now is for us to have a system that ensures democratic participation until such time as we get, through economic development, especially industrialization, the crystallization of socio-economic groups upon which we can then base healthy political parties."[99] As pointed out by the scholar Nelson Kasfir, the characterization of the movement system as transitional, pending sufficient economic development before a return to multiparty politics, can easily serve as a justification for the indefinite political domination by the movement system. Kasfir rightly asks:

Museveni has not offered even a rough idea of when this day will arrive. How long will it take for Uganda's peasants to become members of the working or middle class? Is the NRM saying that it must remain the

---

[98]Nelson Kasfir, "Uganda politics and the Constituent Assembly Elections of March 1994," in Hansen and Twaddle, *From Chaos to Order*, p. 149. Law Professor Frederick Jjuuko made a similar claim to Human Rights Watch:

There are two things one needs to know about the NRM in Uganda. First is the history of militarism which is still with us today. The NRM is a semi-militaristic regime both in outlook and its problem-solving techniques. The constitutional arrangements are basically a cover-up of this military arrangement. Second, the proffered excuse for the movement is that parties are ethnic and sectarian, but the movement is equally ethnically based. It is basically southern, or even more narrowly south-west based. Most critical positions are held by people from this region. So the movement has the same shortcomings as the political parties.

Human Rights Watch interview with Professor Frederick Jjuuko, chair, Free Movement, Kampala, April 14, 1998.
[99]Museveni, *Sowing the Mustard Seed*, p. 195.

guardian of no-party democracy until that happens? What seems disturbingly clear is that the NRM has abandoned any ground on which it could lay plausible claim to democratic legitimation, and now seeks to justify its rule on the basis of a highly suspect theory of modernization.[100]

The actions of NRM leaders do not suggest that the movement system is seriously contemplating a transition to a multiparty system. Instead, the NRM continues to move towards an increased institutional entrenchment of the movement system and its own leaders' predominance.

The Constitutional Restrictions on Political Rights

Article 269 of the 1995 constitution entrenched a number of restrictions on political activity which remain in force. It is envisioned in the constitution that these restrictions ultimately will be fully implemented by a law regulating political activity in Uganda. A draft political organizations bill, discussed below, is currently under consideration in parliament. Although article 269 of the constitution allows political parties to exist in name, their activities are almost completely curtailed. Article 269 prohibits their:

(a) opening and operating branch offices;

(b) holding delegates' conferences;

(c) holding public rallies;

(d) sponsoring or offering a platform to or in any way campaigning for or against a candidate for any public election;

---

[100]Kasfir, "'No-Party Democracy' in Uganda," p. 61. Joe Oloka-Onyango, dean of Makerere University Law School, pointed out to Human Rights Watch that the NRM's justification for a ban on political activity had changed over time: "The initial justification for the parties ban was the need for a cooling off period. Then Museveni developed the theory that we were a peasant society not ready for multiparty competition, suggesting a much longer model of transition." Human Rights Watch interview with Joe Oloka-Onyango, Kampala, April 14, 1998.

(e) carrying on any activities that may interfere with the movement political system for the time being in force.[101]

The passage of article 269 in June 1995 led to a walk out from the constituent assembly by most advocates of pluralism, popularly known as "multipartyists."[102] DP leader Paul Ssemogerere explained to Human Rights Watch that he participated in the walk-out because he felt that article 269 finally exposed the real motives of the Museveni government:

> We walked out of the constituent assembly over article 269. It was clear progressively that the true colors of Museveni came out: he would not compromise on the movement and marketed the movement as a political system when it really is a one party rule. You build a party which is identical to the state and use state resources, councils and the administration to perpetuate it. You bring in the security bodies and ensure they are behind you.[103]

Major General Tinyefuza and Lieutenant Colonel Lwanga, two outspoken NRA delegates who advocated a return to a more pluralistic society at the constituent assembly, again showed their disagreement with the movement stance by publicly abstaining from voting on article 269.

The drafters of article 269 argue that it is based on the desires of the population, which they claim was consulted during the constitution drafting process. Justice Kanyeihamba, presidential advisor on international and human rights affairs from 1992 until 1997, and a member of the constituent assembly, justified the restrictions in Article 269 to Human Rights Watch in these terms:

> The 269 restrictions are in the constitution and were discussed at the constituent assembly. The general feeling was that if we would have had a referendum then, the people of Uganda would have wanted the parties banned for ten years or more. The population felt very strongly that multipartyism should never return to Uganda. I want you to remember

---

[101]Constitution, Article 269.

[102]The label of "multipartyist" and "movementist" are in wide circulation in Uganda, and frequently one of the first facts mentioned to Human Rights Watch when discussing any person was his or her affiliation with the one or the other.

[103]Human Rights Watch interview with Paul Ssemogerere, President, Democratic Party, Mengo, Uganda, May 7, 1998.

that it was against this background that the provisions of the constitution were inserted. We reflected the wishes of the people as delegates at the constituent assembly.[104]

The opposition politicians and advocates for pluralism interviewed by Human Rights Watch viewed the restrictions contained in article 269 as effectively curtailing political opposition in Uganda. Dr. James Rwanyarare, chairperson of the presidential policy commission of the UPC, told Human Rights Watch: "We are in political exile within Uganda. We cannot hold meetings or do anything which may interfere with the NRM. We can have a national office and issue statements but we are not allowed to step out of this office and participate in the politics of the country."[105] Norbert Mao, an outspoken member of parliament from northern Uganda, described article 269 as a "time bomb," a danger to the future stability of Uganda: "We have some time bombs in our constitution, this article 269 which turns political parties into scarecrows. The President says parties are not banned but they can't compete for power, so what are parties for?"[106] According to Aggrey Awori, an MP from Busia, the restrictions of article 269 create a political climate similar to that of a one-party state: "Article 269 of the constitution restricts political parties. As a result, the NRM has entrenched itself to the total disadvantage of other political activists. Multipartyists do not have the opportunity or resources to campaign in the same way as movementists."[107]

The Movement Act: A State-Sponsored Political Party in Disguise

The Local Council System
    During its guerrilla campaign against the second Obote government, the NRA/M established resistance councils (RC) in the villages under its control, as well as some similar but clandestine structures in contested areas. These structures were loosely based on the neighborhood committees organized in the "liberated

---

[104]Human Rights Watch interview with Justice Prof. G.W. Kanyeihamba, justice of supreme court of Uganda and former presidential advisor on international and human rights affairs (1992-97), Mengo, Uganda, May 8, 1998.
    [105]Human Rights Watch interview with Dr. James Rwanyarare, chairperson, presidential policy commission, Uganda Peoples Congress, Kampala, April 8, 1998.
    [106]Human Rights Watch interview with Norbert Mao MP (Gulu Municipality), Kampala, April 8, 1998.
    [107]Human Rights Watch interview with Aggrey Awori MP (Busia), Kampala, April 6, 1998.

zones" of Mozambique by the Front for the Liberation of Mozambique (FRELIMO) in the late 1960s.[108] Although originally designed as support structures for the NRA fighters, the resistance councils grew into a model for what was viewed as "popular democracy." When the NRA/M came into power in 1986, it sought to spread the institution nation-wide as the basis for its administration.

The resistance councils—renamed local councils in 1997—start at the village level (LC1), and progress through the parish (LC2) to the sub-county (LC3), county (LC4), and district (LC5). During the early period of NRM rule, the national government's legislative branch was the un-elected National Resistance Council (NRC), which was replaced in 1996 by a largely directly elected parliament in which a number of nonelected seats were reserved for the army and other government sectors and interest groups which tend to be NRM-aligned. Originally, elections to the LC1 council involved villagers publicly lining up behind candidates, a practice which has now been abandoned in favor of a secret ballot.

The degree of participatory democracy the local councils provided at the grassroots levels contrasted sharply with the lack of such popular participation at the national level. Mahmood Mamdani, the former chairperson of a government commission appointed by the NRM in 1987 to study local government in Uganda, concludes that "the NRM was unable to link its participatory reform at the village level with a representative reform at higher levels.... The RC system increasingly came to reflect two tiers: one local, the other central; one on the ground, the other at the apex. The higher one went up the RC pyramid, the more watered down was the democratic content of the system."[109]

According to a number of persons interviewed by Human Rights Watch, some of the local council structures serve as partisan NRM bodies during election times and target multipartyists and their supporters for abuse during these periods. Wycliffe Birungi, the chairperson of the human rights committee of the Uganda Law Society, told Human Rights Watch that local councils often mobilized in support of NRM candidates: "Local councils have been used as an organ for purposes of campaigning for politicians, especially for the local MPs and district counsellors belonging to the movement system. The local councils tell the people

---

[108]Museveni, *Sowing the Mustard Seed*, p. 30. Museveni observed the FRELIMO neighborhood committees during his visit to the "liberated zones" as a student at the University of Tanzania in 1968.
[109]Mahmood Mamdani, *Citizen and Subject: Contemporary Africa and the Legacy of Late Colonialism* (Princeton, N.J.: Princeton University Press, 1996), p. 216.

that they want a movement person, and that so and so is a movement person. They can very much influence the success of a candidate."[110]

The National Organization for Civic Education and Elections Monitoring (NOCEM) also complained about the partisan role of local council officials in the 1996 presidential and parliamentary elections.[111] The International Foundation for Election Systems (IFES) found that the local council system was used to mobilize pro-movement support in the 1996 elections:

> [W]hile the LCs and special interest groups are holdovers from an earlier era, they remain extremely useful electoral resources to the Movement because of its control over them. The Resident District Commissioners (RDCs) play an important role in many districts, controlling the electoral colleges representing these special interest groups as well as administering the political mobilizers in each district and the party schools. The RDCs played a partisan role in these elections, as the Interim Electoral Commission recognized in a press release warning them not to support particular parliamentary candidates. The earlier [LC] structures may not carry the same degree of ideological belief as they attracted in 1986, but they provided organizational advantages and a convenient rationale for denying similar resources to multipartyists who oppose the movement.[112]

Discussing the presidential election campaign of 1996, IFES concluded: "If Museveni wanted, as he himself stated, to win a 'fair fight,' many of his local supporters, particularly within the government structure, seem to have directly counteracted his intentions."[113] Paul Ssemogerere, Museveni's main challenger in the 1996 presidential elections, complained to Human Rights Watch about a biased campaign system favoring Museveni:

> The law was against us because we were not allowed to campaign as an organization, but Museveni was using the government machinery to

---

[110]Human Rights Watch interview with Wycliffe Birungi, chairperson, human rights committee of the Uganda Law Society, Kampala, April 10, 1998.

[111]NOCEM, Presidential Elections 1996: Interim Report, p. 4; NOCEM, Parliamentary Elections 1996: Interim Report, p. 5.

[112]International Foundation for Election Systems, *Uganda: Long-Term Observation of 1996 Presidential and Legislative Elections* (Washington, DC: IFES 1996), pp. 65-66.

[113]Ibid., p. 49.

campaign. The RDCs and LC structures were expected to campaign.
Those who did not support Museveni were seen as disloyal and some
were thrown out of their positions in the LC councils.[114]

President Museveni, the incumbent in the 1996 presidential elections, regularly
used his government position to circumvent the campaign rules put in place for the
presidential elections.   In one of the more egregious examples of such
circumvention of campaign rules, Museveni gave a live radio broadcast after the
official campaigning period had ended, warning that Uganda would revert to its
former state of anarchy if the population did not vote for him.[115]

Dr. Rwanyarare, chairperson of the pro-Obote presidential policy commission
of the UPC, told Human Rights Watch that the local council members at the village
level often targeted UPC supporters: "The LC officers are the worst because they
operate on a village level. There are cases where people have been expelled from
villages, so most will not criticize the government because they fear expulsion.
The villagers know that the parties cannot come to their aid, so they comply with
the LC officers who are executive, legislature and judiciary all in one. The LC is
a very powerful weapon which you cannot appeal against."[116]

The local council structures were granted some judicial powers in 1987.[117] In
many districts paramilitary local defense units (LDUs) continue to operate
extralegally, although there is no law providing for their existence. Both the local
council's judicial powers and the local defense units' military powers are
frequently abused, at times against political opponents of the movement system.
According to Wycliffe Birungi, chairperson of the human rights committee of the
Uganda Law Society, local council courts often abuse their powers by handing out
sentences which are beyond their powers, such as corporal punishment and
banishment from the village, and by taking on cases which are beyond their
jurisdiction, such as rape or defilement (statutory rape) cases.[118] Justice Odoki,

---

[114]Human Rights Watch interview with Paul Ssemogerere, President, Democratic
Party, Mengo, May 7, 1998.

[115]Karoli Lwanga Ssemogerere, "Towards a Transparent Electoral System in Uganda:
A Case Study of the Presidential Elections in Uganda, 1996," dissertation (Kampala:
Makerere University, 1997), p. 129.

[116]Human Rights Watch interview with Dr. James Rwanyarare, chairperson,
presidential policy commission, Uganda Peoples Congress, Kampala, April 8, 1998.

[117]Judicial powers were granted by the Resistance Committees (Judicial Powers)
Statute of 1987.

[118]Human Rights Watch interview with Wycliffe Birungi, chairperson, Human Rights
Committee, Uganda Law Society, Kampala, April 10, 1998.

chairperson of the Judicial Service Commission, shared this assessment of the local council courts, stating that they have illegally imposed caning, tried capital cases, and that they lack impartiality.[119]

According to some opposition politicians, the local defense units add a measure of paramilitary coercion in some districts during elections. Patrick Mwonda, a UPC activist, claimed that the LDUs in his district had been mobilized the night before the 1996 parliamentary elections to intimidate his supporters. According to Mwonda,

> In my own district, the LDUs were mobilized on the Wednesday before voting on Thursday, and the LDUs patrolled every village throughout the night of Wednesday. They would go to villages and tell everyone to get out of their homes. They would tell them to sit and surround them with guns, and then they would ask them who they would vote for tomorrow. They would pick out my activists and cane them in front of the population.[120]

During a 1996 campaign meeting of presidential contender Paul Ssemogerere in Mbale, LDU members reportedly fired their rifles in the air in an apparent effort to disperse his supporters.[121]

The Movement Structures

The Movement Act of 1997 creates a second set of structures, essentially duplicating the structures of the local councils (previously known as resistance councils). Like the local councils, the movement structures exist at the village, parish, sub-county, division, and district levels, in addition to the National Movement Conference and its permanent secretariat.[122] The national conference is the highest movement organ, and consists of a national chair and vice-chair, a

---

[119]Human Rights Watch interview with Justice Odoki, chairperson, Judicial Service Commission, April 14, 1998.

[120]Human Rights Watch interview with Patrick Mwhonda, secretary, the interim executive committee, Uganda People's Congress, Kampala, May 9, 1998. See also Richard Okumu Wengi, "Free and Fair Elections and the Question of Voting Rights in Uganda, 1986-1996," in Joe Oloka-Onyango, *A Decade of the National Resistance Movement in Uganda: The Human Rights Balance Sheet* (unpublished manuscript), p. 25, describing the institution of pro-NRM night-time political patrols just prior to the 1996 presidential elections, a practice called *Kakuyege.*

[121]"Uganda: Yoweri rules," *Economist*, April 13, 1996, p. 35.

[122]Movement Act (1997), article 4.

political commissar, all members of parliament, the chairpersons of all division, municipal, town or subcounty movement committees, all resident district commissioners, as well as representatives from women, youth, trade, army, police, prison, business, and veterans.[123]

For members of parliament, membership in the National Conference is mandatory, as is membership of all Ugandans in their village movement council.[124] The compulsory nature of membership in the movement was emphasized by Minister of State for Political Affairs Amama Mbabazi, who told Human Rights Watch: "According to our constitution, the political system we have is the movement system, so that means that everyone belongs to the movement. [Democratic Party President Paul] Ssemogerere belongs to the movement by law, he has no choice."[125]

The purpose of the movement act is unclear from the legislation itself, especially in light of the fact that the movement act virtually duplicates the entire pyramidical structure of local government created by the Local Government Act of 1997. The local councils have some executive, legislative and judicial powers in terms of the current legislation.[126] The local councils are supposed to, among other duties, serve as communication channels between the population and the central government, help in the maintenance of law and order, recruit for the UPDF and security forces, and initiate self-help projects.[127] Each village council (LC1) has a secretary for information, mobilization, and education, as well as a secretary for security and a chairperson who is the political head of the village.[128] In addition to the local council structures, each district is headed by a resident district commissioner (RDC), who serves as the district representative of central government, and whose duties include sensitizing the local populace to national government policies and programs, as well as overseeing the operation of the local councils.[129] With such a comprehensive program of representation at all levels of government, it is difficult to see the role of this second system of structures which essentially duplicates the first—except as a form of partisan party structure normally associated with one-party states.

---

[123]Ibid., article 5.

[124]Ibid., article 5 and article 25.

[125]Human Rights Watch interview with Amama Mbabazi, Minister of State for Political Affairs, Kampala, May 5, 98.

[126]Local Government Act (1997).

[127]Local Government Act (1997), Section 49.

[128]Ibid., Sections 48 and 51.

[129]Ibid., Section 71.

The Movement Act in effect replicates the structures of a political organization that is a party in all but name, the National Resistance Movement, as structures of the Ugandan state, creating a state-sponsored political organization disguised as a "political system." In practice, the principal duty of the movement structures is to mobilize support for the NRM's movement government system and for a vote in favor of the retention of this system in the referendum. This role was previously played by the NRM's own national secretariat—which itself continues to function as the state-funded "Office of Political Mobilization" under the Minister of State for Political Affairs. The movement structures are directly funded by the Ugandan state, creating a state-funded political organization charged with promoting the governing system, to which all Ugandans must belong.

The NRM and its leadership continue to deny that the NRM is a political organization, preferring to describe the movement as a political system rather than a party. But the actions of the NRM and its adherents are little different from those of a political party. NRM members identify themselves as movement or NRM supporters—often making distinctions between "historicals" and newer members. The NRM has a caucus in parliament which formulates the movement position on legislation and other policies under consideration. The NRM actively campaigns for its candidates during elections, with President Museveni himself urging the electorate to vote for movement candidates in the days before the 1998 local government elections:

Let me also remind you that the national programme in place is the programme of the Movement which you supported and elected. Therefore, you need to choose those individuals who will adhere to the movement political and economic programmes which the government has put in place to advance unity, development and progress. ... You should always welcome those who profess to work for the Movement and judge them according to their merit. But they should be professed to support the Movement.[130]

---

[130]"Look for Integrity and Patriotism—Museveni," *New Vision*, April 17, 1998. President Museveni's comments drew an angry response from former presidential candidate Kibirige Mayanja who issued a press statement accusing the president of trying to influence the elections:"It is therefore clear that the Movement is an unjust system intended to give some candidates a privileged position while crippling the others. This has revealed the true colours of the movement as a political party." Andrew Mwenda, "Kibirige Mayanja attacks Museveni," *Monitor*, April 18, 1998, p. 2; Karyeija Kagambirwe, "Mayanja raps Museveni election speech," *New Vision*, April 18, 1998, p. 32.

President Museveni also stated at a press conference after the election that senior members of government should only intervene in elections to back a candidate when a multipartyist was contesting against a movement candidate, stating "that is my critical enemy, the one who talks of parties now."[131] President Museveni's views are repeated by countless local government officials, army officers, parliamentarians, and others who urge the local population to vote for movement candidates. As the resident district commissioner of Kasese told Human Rights Watch, "Officially, officials like us condemn the multipartyists and people are starting to understand. The UPC was strongest in the west. This is the argument we are using: all these conflicts we see today have their roots in the multipartyist."[132]

In the face of a number of electoral set-backs for the NRM in the 1998 local government elections—many important positions were won by multipartyist candidates associated with political parties, including the mayorship of the capital Kampala—it appears that the NRM may move towards even more direct sponsorship of NRM candidates.   In an interview with the *East African*, Professor Gilbert Bukenya, the chair of the movement caucus in parliament, stated that the NRM would in future screen movement candidates and would offer only one candidate to prevent dividing the vote between different movement candidates: "Multipartyist have been exploring our weakness, which has made numerous movement candidates end up dividing their votes."[133]   When interviewed by Human Rights Watch, Minister of State for Political Affairs Mbabazi first attempted to distinguish the movement from political parties by suggesting that only the political parties sponsor candidates. When the minister was asked to comment on the statement by Professor Bukenya that the NRM was instituting similar practices, he told Human Rights Watch:

> We must sort out what to do in such cases as the recent local council elections in Kampala, where the vote can be split between different movement candidates. There is a dilemma because parties are not supposed to sponsor candidates, because we want to avoid tribal voting. When parties sit and act as parties to choose candidates, the choice we

---

[131]J.B. Wasswa and John Kakande, "Museveni Speaks out on Sebaggala," *New Vision*, April 22, 1998, at p. 2.

[132]Human Rights Watch interview with Yorokamu K. Kamacerere, Resident District Commissioner of Kasese, April 17, 1998.

[133]James Kigozi, "One Candidate Only, Says Defeated NRM," *East African*, April 27-May 3, 1998, at p. 1.

have is to act in a unified way. What do we do? In that event, maybe we shall also organize against them. We can crack down and use the law against them or organize ourselves politically against the parties.[134]

Most of the advocates for pluralism interviewed by Human Rights Watch shared the view that the NRM was trying to entrench itself in power by creating structures that made the NRM synonymous with the state. Karuhanga K. Chapaa, chairperson of the National Democrats Forum, told Human Rights Watch:

> The NRM is a party, trying to steal members of other parties and break down other parties. There is a failure on the part of the NRM to look for partnerships in the process of democratization. ... Now the NRM structures are state organs used to dominate society in the same way as the Communist Party. Everybody must belong to the movement. Even as a minority we should be allowed to exist. They feel they are strong, militarily superior and they know the parties don't have an army. Democracy includes readiness to accept defeat and leave power, but the NRM doesn't accept this.[135]

Law professor Frederick Jjuuko agreed: "We really became a one-party state because the movement is organized as any party, and it uses state resources while denying others freedom of association."[136]

The one factor which distinguishes the movement system from the previous generation of one-party states in Africa—including the one-party state created by President Julius Nyerere in Tanzania from which the NRM has drawn significant inspiration[137]—is that the movement defines itself as a political system, not a

---

[134]Human Rights Watch interview with Amama Mbabazi, Minister of State for Political Affairs, Kampala, May 5, 98.

[135]Human Rights Watch interview with Karuhanga K. Chapaa, Chairperson, National Democrats Forum Party, Kampala, April 7, 1998.

[136]Human Rights Watch interview with Frederick Jjuuko, Makerere University Law Professor, Kampala, April 14, 1998.

[137]Nelson Kasfir discusses the similarities in thinking between Nyerere and Museveni in a recent essay. Nyerere also justified his one-party state on the belief that African societies were not divided along social and economic lines, and that parties would only encourage "factionalism." Nyerere argued that his Tanganyika African National Union (TANU) party was open to all Tanzanians, thus guaranteeing free and fair elections. Kasfir, "'No-Party Democracy' in Uganda," p. 60.

political party, despite having most of the characteristics of a political party.[138] The reason for this semantic difference in definition is two-fold.

First, the NRM has a sophisticated world outlook, and realizes that declaring Uganda a one-party state would lead to a significant loss of international support. Declaring Uganda a one-party state would place international donors and allies such as European Union members and the United States in a difficult and embarrassing position of closely supporting a declared one-party state and could lead to a withdrawal of political or financial support by some donor nations. Instead, the NRM has managed to achieve political dominance through a careful manipulation of the political system and an occasional resort to coercive measures, while retaining their international support. This is an analysis echoed by Professor Akiiki Mujaju of Makerere University:

> It is not fashionable today to talk of one-party systems, and therefore new methods of concealing them have to be found. The NRM is no different from many one-party systems with which we are familiar. It is in government, has a secretariat which is busy indoctrinating people, and has leaders, although the selection process for those leaders is not transparent.[139]

Second, by refusing to define itself as a political party, the NRM has been able to operate freely while denying the same freedom of operation to the opposition political parties which are strictly controlled under article 269 of the constitution. The NRM feels free to support and sponsor movement candidates, to hold public rallies, and to engage in all the activities which it refuses to allow political parties to engage in. Thus, the NRM gets the best of both worlds.

The NRM's critique of political parties in Uganda serves as its primary justification for the continued reliance on the movement system of government. Without the movement system of government, the NRM and Museveni argue, the country will once again be plunged into chaos and anarchy. However, it is difficult

---

[138]One of the notable differences between the NRM's administration and earlier one-party states in Africa is that the NRM does not claim to advocate a political ideology but presents itself as multi-ideological. Many earlier one-party states in Africa were identified with a strong party ideology, such as *ujamaa* or African socialism (Tanzania) or African humanism (Zambia).

[139]Akiiki B. Mujaju, "Civil Society at Bay in Uganda," in Georges Nzongola-Ntalaja and Margaret C. Lee (eds.), *The State and Democracy in Africa* (Trenton, NJ: Africa World Press, 1997), p. 50.

to see what distinguishes the NRM from the political parties it criticizes so severely, as pointed out by Ugandan academic Mahmood Mamdani:

> [T]he NRM's critique of political parties falls short on one count: lacking an element of self-criticism, it tends to be self-serving. For if the parties have turned into breeding grounds for individuals who turn to politics as the quickest road to position and privilege, so is the NRM fast becoming so. If party programmes are more a public relations exercise than a policy pledge, so does the NRM's 10-point programme [which is] honoured less in practice than in the breach, more a litany for ceremonial occasions than a guide for day-to-day action. If the parties do not have an internal constitution that allows the membership to hold the leadership accountable, neither does the NRM. If the parties are mainly funded by a few wealthy individuals and institutions, local or foreign, the NRM is also fast becoming mainly a state-funded body. The sad fact is that the NRM is today fast moving on the same track that UPC and DP have covered since independence; it is on its way to becoming a state movement.[140]

Elections for the movement structures outlined in the 1997 Movement Act took place in July 1998. The national movement conference which selected the national movement leadership consisted of more than 1600 delegates, but the selection process ensured that most delegates were movement supporters.[141] President Museveni, who has been chairperson of the NRM since its creation, was elected chairperson of the movement unopposed. Al-hajji Moses Kigongo, vice-chair of the NRM since its creation, was elected unopposed as vice-chair of the

---

[140]Mahmood Mamdani, "Pluralism and the Right of Association," in Mahmood Mamdani and Joe Oloka-Onyango, *Uganda: Studies in Living Conditions, Popular Movements and Constitutionalism* (Vienna: Austrian Journal of Development Studies, 1994), p. 556.

[141]The national conference of the movement consists of all members of parliament; all RDCs; all members of every district executive committee; the chairpersons of all division, municipal, subcounty and town council movement committees; ten representatives of the UPDF; five representatives each from the National Women's Executive Committee, the National Youth Executive Committee, the National Organization of Trade Unions, the National Association of Disabled Persons, the Uganda Police Force and the Veterans' Association; three representatives of the Uganda Prison Services; and ten representatives of the private business sector. Many seats were thus reserved either for organs created by the movement act, or interest groups closely aligned with or organized by the NRM.

movement.[142] In effect, the movement elections allowed the NRM to transform itself into a state-funded political party without diluting its hold on power. The government-owned *New Vision* quoted President Museveni as saying that his unopposed appointment was "a better arrangement than last time [the presidential elections] when I had to fight [opposition presidential contender] Ssemogerere."[143]

The National Executive Committee (NEC) of the movement, chaired by Museveni and dominated by NRM adherents, then proceeded to meet in a series of closed, private sessions to select the national political commissar and directors of the movement secretariat. Museveni told the *New Vision* that he had selected Speaker of Parliament James Wapakhabulo as national political commissar because "Parliament has got a limited job.... We need more of our cadres to mobilize the population."[144] Museveni also announced that the vice chairman of the movement, Hajji Moses Kigongo, would receive a salary equivalent to that of Uganda's vice president, that the national political commissar would receive the same salary as the speaker of parliament, and that the directors of the movement secretariat would be paid at the same rate as ministers of state.[145] The NEC later announced that it adopted rules which prohibit members from disclosing any information discussed in the closed sessions, continuing a long tradition of secrecy and intrigue surrounding the functioning of NRM structures.[146]

Mahmood Mamdani, professor of African Studies at the University of Cape Town, commented that the movement elections were another step in the creation of a one-party state:

> With these structures, [the NRM] which used to be only a secretariat in Kampala, will now be a ruling party.... We will eventually have a single party—called a movement—and a single party which will organize a referendum every five years and organize support for its legitimacy.[147]

---

[142]Ofwono Opondo, "Museveni seeks MP's votes for the chair," *New Vision*, July 12, 1998; Robert Mukasa and Pius Muteekani Katunzi, "Museveni, Kigongo take top movement jobs," *Monitor*, July 14, 1998.

[143]"Museveni, Wapa picked," *New Vision*, July 14, 1998.

[144]"No Ceasefire, Says Museveni," *New Vision*, July 22, 1998, p.1.

[145]Henry Ochieng, "Parties will die, says President," *Monitor*, July 22, 1998.

[146]John Kakande, "National Conference Proceedings not to be disclosed," *New Vision*, July 20, 1998.

[147]Paul Busharizi, "Uganda's Museveni to Head Umbrella 'Movement,'" Reuters, July 13, 1998.

The comments of the newly elected movement leadership themselves suggest that they see the movement structures as a political organization. James Wapakhabulo, the newly elected National Political Commissar, initially refused to resign his position as speaker of parliament on the grounds that the position was not a public but a political office:

> The Secretariat ... is a political organ within the Movement political system. It is not part of government. Offices in the movement political system are political offices. They are not public service offices within the meaning of the Constitution.[148]

Members of the movement secretariat are required to closely adhere to NRM doctrine and policies. The outspoken anti-corruption crusader Winnie Byanyima, appointed director of information in the movement secretariat, was fired in February 1999 by President Museveni, acting in his capacity as chairperson of the movement. A statement by President Museveni explained the reasons for the firing:

> The movement chairman [President Museveni] regretted that despite his advice to Honorable Winnie Byanyima that in her capacity as the movement director of information she should refrain from taking a position contrary to the official stand and policy of the movement, she had failed to comply.[149]

Chaka-mchaka: Political Education for Social Control?

One of the tools used by the NRM government to increase its political control, targeted particularly at civil servants and graduating students, is a political education and military science course called *Chaka-mchaka*, a term which mimics the sound made by military boots during marches. Supporters of pluralism in Uganda object to chaka-mchaka on the grounds that it is a disguised program of political indoctrination into the NRM's ideology, including the belief that political parties are at the root of Uganda's past troubles. According to Democratic Party leader Paul Ssemogerere, "Chaka-mchaka is supposedly a military training

---

[148]John Kakande, "Wapa Refuses to Quit," *New Vision*, July 27, 1998. Wapakhabulo later resigned his post of speaker of the house. "Wapa, Ayume Quit," *New Vision*, July 28, 1998.

[149]"Uganda: NRM Information Director Dismissed," *Radio Uganda*, February 19, 1999.

program for community self-defense. It is actually a political program, an
indoctrination into hating democratic pluralism and a constant reminder of the
skeletons of the conflicts of the past." Law professor Jjuuko of Makerere
University expressed a similar opinion of the courses: "The program would include
the following two elements. First, there was the demystification of the gun [i.e.,
teaching the population not to fear guns]. Second, there was the political
education, which included a history of Uganda according to the NRM, a crude form
of historical materialism, and placed the blame for Uganda's past woes on the
political parties."[150] Because chaka-mchaka includes indoctrination into the belief
that political parties are responsible for Uganda's past problems, it serves to justify
the restrictions on political rights in effect today.

The systematic political education of its cadres and the general population has
deep roots in the NRA/M movement, dating back to the earliest days of its guerrilla
struggle. As early as 1971, Museveni instituted political education as one of the
main training components of the Front for National Salvation (FRONESA) he was
then leading, and the presence of Political Commissars at all levels of the UPDF
continue this tradition to date. Museveni viewed his army as a "people's army" and
his soldiers as "politicians in uniform," and claimed that the politicization of his
rebel soldiers led to an increased respect for the human rights of civilians.[151] The
NRM extended its political education courses to the general population as it gained
control over Ugandan territory. Mobile schools of political education operated
during the guerrilla war, explaining the aims of the NRA/M, and were transformed
in 1986 into a permanent institution, the National School of Political Education.[152]
The Special District Administrators appointed by the NRM government to establish
the local council system relied heavily on graduates of the National School of
Political Education to politically educate local populations.[153] The value of the
political education program for entrenchment of the NRM ideology and
administration was not lost, as described by one senior NRA officer:

> Quite apart from educating people about the aims and objectives of the
> NRM, political education was also a very effective way of winning

---

[150]Human Rights Watch interview with Frederick Jjuuko, Makerere University Law
Professor, Kampala, April 14, 1998.
[151]Ofcansky, *Uganda*, p. 54.
[152]Amaza, *Museveni's Long March*, p. 154. According to the late Ondoga, a senior
officer of the NRA, the school moved locations from Namugongo to Wakiso and later to
Kyankwanzi.
[153]Ibid.

support for the movement. The establishment of the RCs [resistance councils] and the institution of political education thus came to be seen, especially by the UPC and DP, as a threat to their existence. Right from the outset, forces associated with these parties were vehemently opposed to RCs and political education, claiming the former were communist structures, and the latter communist indoctrination. There was, however, no deterring the NRM-NRA from establishing RCs or spreading political education to all corners of the country.[154]

According to the inspector-general of government, Jotham Tumwesigye, the NRM national secretariat received a budget allocation from the government, used partly to fund a school for political training.[155] Resident District Commissioners were provided with funding for chaka-mchaka, and political education was considered one of their major responsibilities, although these programs were periodically suspended due to lack of money. Civil servants were required to take the courses:

> Civil servants used to go for one month to Budo to receive political education and military training. In the morning you start with chaka-mchaka at 6 a.m. At 10 a.m. the political lectures begin.[156]

Law professor Jjuuko gave a similar description of chaka-mchaka to Human Rights Watch:

> In terms of school teachers, it was expected that you attend the courses, and the same was expected from people in the parastatals and civil servants. They wanted to extend it to the university but they failed to force it on us in 1989. Students who are entering their first year would be called to go to political school before entering university and the bulk of them went. This is still in place, but people now know that they don't have to attend to be admitted to the university. Now, probably 50 or 60 percent attend, while in 1993 it was probably 90 percent. Upcountry, at

---

[154]Ibid., p. 155.

[155]Human Rights Watch interview with Jotham Tumwesigye, inspector-general of government, Kampala, May 7, 1998.

[156]Ibid.

the village level, the self-defense military training would be mixed with political education.[157]

Karuhanga K. Chapaa, chairperson of the National Democrats Forum Party, described the political education program as indoctrination:

> They take people for indoctrination classes just like the Communist Party. They come and go to the rural area and seek out the influential people, the powerful people. They start indoctrinating them in the NRM ideology, about the crimes of political parties and multipartyists. Then the influential people carry out local courses. Even university students attend such courses. They try and reach everybody.[158]

Under the new constitutional dispensation, the NRM national secretariat which was responsible for political education is supposed to be disbanded, and its functions transferred to the department of political mobilization in the president's office. According to the minister of state in charge of the department of political mobilization, the constitutional change has merely incorporated the NRM national secretariat into the government structure as the department of political mobilization, a further indication of the continuing convergence between NRM and state structures.

Chaka-mchaka was suspended during the 1996 presidential and parliamentary elections period by the interim electoral commission, following complaints by multiparty supporters and Western diplomats that the courses were giving an unfair advantage to the NRM. President Museveni reportedly announced in August 1997 in Fort Portal that the courses would resume to help consolidate stability in Uganda.[159]

Reports in the *Monitor* newspaper in October 1997 claimed that local leaders and members of the local defense units (LDUs) went house to house in areas of the Masaka district to ensure that all adult members of local villages participated in chaka-mchaka courses.[160] In November 1997, Gertrude Njuba, director of the

---

[157]Human Rights Watch interview with Frederick Jjuuko, Makerere University Law Professor, Kampala, April 14, 1998.

[158]Human Rights Watch interview with Karuhanga K. Chapaa, chairperson, National Democrats Forum Party, Kampala, April 7, 1998.

[159]Editorial, "ChakaMchaka should resume," *New Vision*, August 4, 1997.

[160]Ahmed Musoga and P. Matsiko wa Mucoori, "Mchaka mchaka no longer voluntary," *Monitor*, October 6, 1997.

department of mass mobilization, officiated at a ceremony at the end of a three-week chaka-mchaka course for sixty-two persons, stating that "when one sees the advantages of chaka-mchaka, he or she participates without being forced."[161] After a brutal massacre by rebels of the Allied Democratic Front in western Uganda,[162] Vice President Dr. Specioza Kazibwe announced that chaka-mchaka political and military education efforts in western Uganda would be increased.[163]

Chaka-mchaka courses were further revived in the aftermath of the July 1998 local elections, and the NRM is gearing up to use chaka-mchaka political education to influence the outcome of the referendum in the year 2000. On his appointment as national political commissar, former Speaker of Parliament James Wapakhabulo reportedly said that he would produce cadres through the National School of Political Education to "market" movement ideas among the Ugandan people.[164] On July 24, 1998, the new national political commissar announced that a "massive political education and military science programme" would take place at the National School of Political Education in Kyankwanzi in August 1998:

> The office of the NPC at the Movement Secretariat confirms that a cadre development course for senior six leavers of 1998, shall commence at the National School for Political Education, Kyankwazi on August 7, 1998. This is therefore to inform the concerned senior six leavers to register with the RDC's offices with immediate effect.[165]

The government-owned *New Vision* reported on August 10, 1998 that 500 students had been enrolled in the political education course at Kyankwazi. The course signaled the re-introduction of a systemic chaka-mchaka course after a two-year recess, and each Ugandan district was required to send a minimum of ten students to the course.[166]

---

[161]Meddie Musisi, "Sinners cannot see good side of Movement—Njuba," *Monitor*, September 23, 1997.

[162]See Human Rights Watch, "Human Rights Watch Condemns Deadly Attack By Ugandan Rebels On School Children," June 10, 1998.

[163]Moses Sserwanga, "Kichwamba deaths: Government accepts blame," *Africa News Service*, June 13, 1998.

[164]Pius Muteekani Katunzi & Robert Mukasa, "Wapakhabulo is new Movement NPC," *Monitor*, July 13, 1998.

[165]Alfred Wasike, "Wapa opens Political Education," *New Vision*, July 24, 1998.

[166]Hassan Matovu, "500 Attend Kyankwanzi Course," *New Vision*, August 10, 1998.

Violations of the Right to Freedom of Association

The emphasis on the right to freedom of association as a right to engage in *effective* association *in community with others* is of crucial importance in the context of Uganda, and points out the incompatibility of the restrictions contained in article 269 of the constitution with the right to association. Although article 269 allows parties to exist in name, it effectively deprives them of their essential purpose for being, by prohibiting them from engaging in any way in a contest for political power. As noted, article 269 prohibits political parties from "opening and operating branch offices," "holding delegates' conferences," "holding public rallies," "sponsoring or offering a platform to or in any way campaigning for or against a candidate for public office," and "carrying on any activities that may interfere with the movement political system for the time being in force."

The NRM has vigorously enforced article 269's restrictions on civil and political rights. Activists of the Democratic Party and the Uganda Peoples Congress were repeatedly arrested in 1997 for attempting to sell membership cards to their constituents. According to Democratic Party President Ssemogerere, Minister for Constitutional Affairs Emmanuel Kirenga justified this action on the grounds of article 269(e), which prohibits any interference with the operation of the movement system.[167]

Discussing the upcoming movement elections, Minister of State for Political Affairs Amama Mbabazi told reporters in May, 1998:

> We know there are some people who don't subscribe to the Movement system of government. But it is also true that the country is currently governed under this system. Everybody is in the Movement and will remain so unless [the law] changes. [Kampala's multipartyist mayor] Sebaggala has no choice. He is automatically a member of the [Movement] electoral college for Kampala district.[168]

The requirement of the 1997 Movement Act compelling all members of parliament specifically, and all Ugandans generally to belong to the Movement political

---

[167] Article 269(e) prohibits "carrying on any activities that may interfere with the movement political system for the time being in force." Paul Ssemogerere, "The Political Organization Draft Bill (1997): Is it Healthy for the Political Environment of Uganda, Present and Future?" (March 21, 1998), p. 8.

[168]Michael Sentongo, "Partists Invited to Movement," *New Vision*, May 27, 1998.

system and its structures[169] violates the right to choose *not* to belong to any particular association. As discussed by legal scholar Manfred Nowak:

> It follows from the emphasis on freedom in Art. 22(1) that no one may be forced, either directly or indirectly, by the State or by private parties, to join a political party, a religious society, a commercial undertaking, or a sports club.[170]

As this report makes clear, the movement system, despite its claims to the contrary, has many of the characteristics of a one-party system. The compulsory membership in the movement organs is incompatible with the right to freedom of association.

Because article 72(2) of the constitution allows only for parties that are registered in accord with legislation that has yet been enacted, new political parties cannot legally be formed and operate in Uganda today. Article 270 of the constitution grandfathers political organizations and parties which were in existence before the constitution: they may continue to exist and operate in conformity with the constitution, including the restrictions of Article 269.[171] Uganda has operated under various bans on political party activity since the formation of the NRM government in 1986 (and similar bans instituted by previous administrations). This continued ban on the formation of new political parties has stifled the development of rejuvenated political institutions in Uganda, and has allowed the same parties which President Museveni describes as responsible for Uganda's past woes to dominate the political spectrum outside the NRM.

Violations of the Right to Freedom of Assembly

Article 269 of the constitution severely restricts the right of freedom of assembly, prohibiting political parties from holding political rallies or delegate conferences. These restrictions are inconsistent with the right to freedom of assembly, as they are not based on any of the grounds for derogation listed in

---

[169]Movement Act (1997), article 5(1) (requiring all members of parliament to belong to the National Conference of the Movement); article 25 (requiring all adult members of a village to belong to the village movement committee).

[170]Nowak, *CCPR Commentary*, p. 385. Nowak continues: "For instance, there is no doubt that former Art. 33 of the Constitution of Zaire, which stated that every citizen was from birth automatically a member of the sole, ruling MPR ("Mouvement populaire de la republique") violated Art. 22."

[171]Uganda Constitution (1995), Article 270.

article 21 of the ICCPR. The blanket ban is inconsistent with the principle of proportionality, which requires that "the type and intensity of an interference be absolutely necessary to attain a purpose."[172] Blanket bans on political rallies and delegate conferences are by definition inconsistent with the requirement that the restrictions are "necessary in a democratic society."[173]

The constitutional ban on political rallies and other such activities has been vigorously implemented in Uganda. Even before the constitutional ban, officials would routinely break up political rallies or deny permits for political rallies to those who sought them. Cecilia Ogwal, then the highest-ranking member in a still united UPC, tried to challenge the restrictions on political rallies by attempting to hold a series of rallies in northern Uganda in 1993. During the first rally in Arua in February 1993, called to attempt to revive the UPC party and seek the views of the population on the proposed draft constitution, Ogwal was arrested and many participants were injured when the police dispersed the crowd.[174] She was released a few hours later without charge. Soon thereafter, Ogwal attempted to address a similar rally in neighboring Nebbi district. Her advance team, sent to make preparations for the rally, was placed under arrest by the military. Upon her arrival, Ogwal went to the office of the assistant district administrator and was met by the entire district security team. The administrator told Ogwal that he had instructions not to let her address any rally. Ogwal described what happened next:

> I insisted I see the instructions myself, but he refused to show them. We later obtained the instructions, which originated from the NRM secretariat, and were signed by Eriya Kategaya, who was at the time the national political commissar of the NRM. The instructions instructed all district administrators not to allow any political leader to hold any political meeting however low profile in their district. At the meeting, the district administrator gave me twelve hours to leave the district, or else he would shoot me as a rebel.[175]

Ogwal proceeded to try to hold a meeting at St. Augustine's Church at Mbale in May 1993. The police arrested sixteen of her followers and charged them with

---

[172]Nowak, *CCPR Commentary*, p. 379.

[173]ICCPR, Article 21.

[174]Human Rights Watch interview with Cecilia Ogwal, Chairperson, Interim Executive Committee of the UPC, Kampala, April 13, 1998.

[175]Ibid.

belonging to an illegal organization.[176] Several police officers were later suspended from duty for allowing Ogwal to address a rally in Mbale.[177]

Such incidents continued after the passing of the constitution and the coming into force of article 269 in 1995. The U.S. Department of State documented at least thirteen rallies, seminars, and other public events organized by opposition politicians which were dispersed or prevented by police that year.[178]

Restrictions are not only imposed on opposition politicians and do not always take the form of a formal ban. In March 1998, a peaceful Kampala march organized by Uganda's Catholic Church to call upon the Museveni government to engage in peace talks with the Lord's Resistance Army (LRA) rebel movement was canceled at the last moment at the request of President Museveni. The UPC had called upon all its members to join the peace rally, and persons interviewed by Human Rights Watch claimed it had been canceled at least in part because the government wanted to prevent the rally from becoming a political event.[179]

The Ugandan authorities often justify their intervention by claiming that the organizers of a rally, meeting, or seminar had failed to inform the appropriate authorities or seek permission for their event. However, there are no clear standards in Ugandan law that require organizers to seek police permission prior to organizing a rally or a seminar. The Police Statute grants the officer-in-charge of police the power to issue orders "directing the conduct of assemblies and processions on public roads or streets or at places of public resort."[180] In addition, if "it comes to the knowledge" of the Inspector-General that an assembly or any procession "on any public road or street or any place of public resort" is being planned, and the Inspector-General has reasonable grounds for believing that the planned assembly or procession is likely to cause a breach of the peace, the Inspector-General may prohibit the assembly or procession "by notice in writing to the person responsible for convening the assembly or forming the procession."[181] These regulations appear to be followed rarely in the cases described below.

---

[176]Ibid.

[177]Ibid.

[178]U.S. Department of State, Bureau of Democracy, Human Rights and Labor, "Uganda Country Report on Human Rights Practices for 1995" (Washington DC: U.S. Dept. of State, 1996).

[179]Human Rights Watch interview, Kampala, April 14, 1998. The same conclusion was reached by the U.S. Department of State, Bureau of Democracy, Human Rights and Labor, "Uganda Country Report on Human Rights Practices for 1997" (Washington DC: U.S. Dept. of State, 1998).

[180]Police Statute (No. 13 of 1994), article 33.

[181]Police Statute, article 33 (2).

In any case, the pattern of intervention by police in such events is clearly arbitrary and selective. Human Rights Watch is not aware of a single case in which pro-movement or NRM events were interfered with by the Ugandan authorities; only those events perceived as being "political" and counter to the movement ideology are targeted. The lack of clear standards about notice and permission requirements for public events allow the Ugandan authorities to act in this arbitrary and selective manner.

President Clinton's March 1998 Visit

According to reports in the government-controlled *New Vision* newspaper, at least two non-violent political protests were broken up or prevented by police around the time of U.S. President Bill Clinton's March 24-25, 1998, visit to Uganda. On March 20, 1998, police dispersed twelve members of the National Freedom Party (NFP) who attempted to organize a hunger strike in Constitution Square intended to show that not all Ugandans supported the movement system. The events organizer, NFP president Herman Ssemuju, was briefly taken into police custody on that day for questioning after defying orders to dissolve the rally which he was addressing. Police officials claimed that the protest had been dispersed because the organizers failed to seek permission for the event, but Ssemuju claimed that the inspector general of police had been informed of the planned event.[182]

On March 25, the Convention for Multiparty Democracy (CMD) attempted to organize a peaceful demonstration at Constitution Square to urge a return to pluralism in Ugandan politics. The interim coordinator of the CMD, member of parliament John Lukyamuzi, called off the demonstration after receiving a letter from the Inspector General of Police John Odomel backed by a visit from two plainclothes police officers at his residence, ordering him not to go ahead with the planned demonstration.[183]

May 1998 Arrests of Members of Parliament

In May 1998, the Ugandan Parliament debated a controversial land bill which was strongly opposed by many Buganda leaders. Human Rights Watch takes no position on the content of the land bill: our concern is with the ability of interested parties to discuss the contents of proposed legislation freely. The Buganda leaders

---

[182]Juliet Nankinga and Peter Okello Jabweli, "Ssemuju rally stopped," *New Vision*, March 21, 1998.
[183]Richard Mutumba, "Multipartyists call off protest demo," *New Vision*, March 26, 1998.

perceived the land bill as a threat to the *mailo* land held in trust by the *Kabaka* or Buganda king, as the bill proposed granting the occupants of this land a more secure form of tenure, thus limiting the powers of the Kabaka over the mailo lands.

The government attempted to muzzle public debate and halt public protests organized in opposition to the bill. A public lecture on the bill sponsored by the Uganda Youth Environment Project (UYEP), planned at Luzira primary school on May 23, was halted before it got started by plainclothes policemen, who claimed they had orders from "higher authorities." Herman Ssemuju, chair of the National Freedom Party, was expected to address the meeting. According to the government-owned *New Vision*, prior notice of the meeting had been given to the police by the organizers.[184]

Two members of parliament from the Buganda area, John Lukyamuzi and Yusuf Nsubuga Nsambu, were arrested and charged with "inciting a rally to do acts calculated to bring death or physical injury" after addressing a May 3, 1998 anti-land bill rally, although no violence resulted.[185] Incitement is a criminal act in terms of the Ugandan criminal code, defined as making to an assembly any statement "indicating or implying that it would be incumbent or desirable ... to do any acts calculated to bring death or physical injury to any person or to any class or community of persons; or to do any acts calculated to lead to the destruction or damage to any property."[186] Lukyamuzi was also charged with "promoting sectarianism." The charges are based on statements made by the two MP's at the rally. Nsambu reportedly told the audience: "Don't think the war we are currently fighting is a joke. It may take a new turn if the land issue does not protect the Baganda." Lukyamuzi reportedly stated: "You should wake up and fight Museveni, even if it means use of arms. You shouldn't sit back as our land is taken, it is our livelihood."[187]

As discussed elsewhere in this report, a radio journalist was detained and questioned for comments he made about the Land Bill. These incidents show the difficulties faced by those who wish to openly challenge controversial government policies. Similar arrests and detentions took place during an October 1996 strike against a newly introduced value-added tax (VAT). After a threat from Interior Minister Tom Butime that the government would arrest people encouraging the continuation of the anti-VAT strike, MP John Lukyamuzi, radio journalist

---

[184]"Land Bill Lecture Stopped," *New Vision*, May 25, 1998.

[185]"Two Uganda Deputies Charged with Incitement to Violence," Agence France Presse, May 7, 1998.

[186]Uganda Penal Code (revised edition 1984), Section 50A.

[187]"Nsambu Hearing Flops," *New Vision*, July 23, 1998.

Mulindwa Muwonge, and at least seven others were arrested and detained overnight by police.[188]

Seminars broken up in June and July 1998

In June and July 1998, a series of peaceful seminars were dispersed by Ugandan authorities. According to the Foundation for African Development (FAD) and Democratic Party (DP) sources and media accounts, on June 19, 1998, police violently dispersed participants in a seminar organized by the Uganda Young Democrats (UYD) and FAD in the Eastern Ugandan town of Tororo. The seminar on "Human Rights and Democracy" was being addressed by Democratic Party President Paul Ssemogerere at the time. According to the administrator of FAD, the organizers had informed the local authorities about the meeting: "FAD and UYD had duly informed district officials in time about the seminar, including the RDC Tororo, Mr. James Magode Ikuya, the police and other local leaders."[189] On the morning of June 19, District Police Commander (DPC) S. P. Tumwesigye called the seminar organizers to his office. According to a participant in that meeting, the organizers were informed that the police were under strict instructions from the RDC to stop the meeting, but the district police commissioner declined to give reasons for the refusal to allow it to be held.[190] Ssemogerere described what happened when the seminar decided to proceed nonetheless:

> At about noon, about sixteen policemen dressed in full riot gear and equipped with shotguns and tear gas canisters and batons took position outside the seminar venue. A few minutes later the [district police commissioner] marched in and ordered the participants to disperse, an order which was ignored by the participants.
>
> Shortly after, we heard a whistle outside the building and baton wielding policemen charged into the building and beat up the participants. One medical doctor [Charles Kasozi] was badly injured around his eye which sustained a serious cut and he had to receive medical attention immediately. Five other participants also received

---

[188]"Ugandan traders defy order to return to work," Reuters World Service, October 4, 1996; "President releases MP, others, held over VAT strike," BBC Summary of World Broadcasts, October 5, 1996.

[189]Statement by Anthony Ssekweyama, administrator, Foundation for African Development, "Facts about the Tororo FAD Seminar," dated July 15, 1998.

[190]Ibid.

injuries from relentless batons. All our protests about the arbitrariness and the high handedness of the unwarranted police intervention fell on deaf ears as the room was cleared.[191]

According to Ssemogerere, the seminar was an entirely peaceful assembly and there was no threat of violence, disruption or breach of the peace to warrant such a violent police response.[192] The incident was similarly described by international media sources.[193]

A second seminar organized by FAD under the same topic, "Democracy and Human Rights," which was due to take place in Kamuli district on July 6, 1998, was declared illegal by District Internal Security Officer (DISO) Lieutenant Baguma, reportedly on orders of the Deputy RDC Martha Asiimwe. The priest in charge of the original venue of the seminar, originally scheduled at Wesunire Catholic Parish Hall, was reportedly asked by the RDC and DISO officials to explain why he had allowed "multipartyists" to use the property.[194] When the organizers attempted to move the seminar to the Umbrella Pub within Kamuli town, they arrived to find the place empty and surrounded by security officials:

At 10:30 a.m., we went straight to Umbrella Pub only to find empty chairs. The hall had been surrounded by plaincloth[es] security operatives. Would-be participants had been told not to go near Umbrella Pub [or face] harassment from the security men.[195]

A FAD representative claimed that Lieutenant Baguma told him: "You always go under cover of this FAD, but these topics have political implications, so we cannot accept you having such a seminar when the police is not aware."[196] The FAD organizers had sought and obtained prior permission from the deputy RDC to hold the seminar. When asked to provide a legal basis for their actions, the security

---

[191] Paul Ssemogerere, "Press Statement: The NRM grows Paranoid, Stops FAD Seminar," dated June 19, 1998. This version of events was confirmed by Ssemogerere in a telephone interview with Human Rights Watch, June 20, 1998.

[192] Human Rights Watch telephone interview with Paul Ssemogerere, President, Democratic Party, June 20, 1998.

[193] "Police Break Up Opposition Meeting in Eastern Uganda," Agence France Presse, June 19, 1998.

[194] Sebuliba Hannington, Manager, Education and Training, FAD, "Eye Witness Account of Kamuli Foiled FAD Seminar," July 7, 1998.

[195] Ibid.

[196] Ibid.

officials were reportedly unable to do so, simply stating that they were acting on the orders of the RDC.[197]

On July 10, 1998, a third seminar organized by the same organizations, with more than one hundred participants, was dispersed at Mbarara, when police officers arrived at the venue and ordered the meeting dispersed on the orders of the district police commander.[198] District Police Commander Fred Nabongo was quoted in the *New Vision* as stating that the organizers had not informed the police and local authorities about their intention to hold the meeting, and claimed that "[t]his meeting was illegal and was likely to cause a breach of the peace."[199] DP President Paul Ssemogerere, who was present at the meeting, vigorously challenged this version of events, claiming that the meeting was entirely peaceful and that the organizers had informed the authorities: "The resident district commissioner and the district police commander were informed in writing and in person long before the seminar. On Thursday, we sent an advance team which got assurances from the local authorities that everything would proceed okay."[200] Anthony Ssekweyama, an organizer of the meeting, also said that the relevant authorities had been informed and had given their permission:

> The first communication with the DPC was in form of an invitation letter to him to attend the FAD/UYD seminar that was to run from 9th to 11th July, 1998. When our co-ordinator in Mbarara served the DPC with this letter, he complained that he should not be invited before he is formally informed as the DPC of the area. When the second letter was delivered ... the DPC said we could go ahead. According to [the Mbarara co-ordinator], he asked the DPC to reply to the letter in writing, and the RDC said it was not necessary. Copies of the letters to the DPC were produced [at the seminar] but he said they were no longer of use to him.[201]

---

[197]Ibid.

[198]Human Rights Watch telephone interview with Paul Ssemogerere, President, Democratic Party, July 14, 1998.

[199]Darius Magara, "Ssemogerere chased away," *New Vision*, July 12, 1998.

[200]Human Rights Watch telephone interview with Paul Ssemogerere, President, Democratic Party, July 14, 1998.

[201]Statement by Anthony Ssekweyama, Administrator, FAD, "Police Breaks up Mbarara FAD/UYD Seminar," (July 15, 1998).

A fourth UYD/FAD workshop on the topic of "Democracy and Human Rights" at Uganda Martyrs University near Masaka, was dispersed by police officials on July 23, 1998. According to Jessica Crowe, a representative of the British Labour Party who was observing the meeting, a group of about fifteen armed police officers surrounded the meeting during the early afternoon and ordered the participants to disperse. The police chief could not state under which law the meeting was being dispersed, and told the UYD leadership that he was acting on orders from higher up. Two plainclothes security agents were present and were identified by the UYD representatives as internal security organization (ISO) agents. Crowe was later informed by the UYD organizers that as the delegates went to their rooms to gather their belongings, police men began stripping branches from nearby trees, and then chased the delegates from the campus by whipping them with the branches. Some delegates were chased all the way to Nkozi town by the police, a distance of several miles. The violent dispersal of the seminar was deplored by the director of the university.[202]

A political rally sponsored by the UYD at Mbarara on July 21, 1998, to protest recent interference with FAD/UYD seminars, was blocked by a heavy police presence, despite the fact that the UYD informed police beforehand of the scheduled event and invited senior district officials and the police to attend.[203]

Seminars Disrupted in July and August 1998

On July 25, 1998, police dispersed a public lecture at the Islamic University in which the Young Congress of Uganda, a UPC-aligned youth group, was presenting a paper entitled "The Land Act: Winners and Losers." Police claimed that they had not been informed of the meeting, and that it thus was illegal.[204]

In another telling incident, a seminar sponsored by the Foundation for Human Rights Initiative (FHRI) in Masindi on July 27, 1998, was interrupted when the RDC entered the venue together with several armed UPDF soldiers, reportedly stating that "I warned Anthony Ssekweyama not to bring his political party

---

[202]Human Rights Watch telephone interview with Jessica Crowe, representative of the British Labour Party, August 18, 1998. See also Ssemujju Ibrahim, "Police hunts UYD out of Nkozi varsity," *Monitor*, July 27, 1998; Kimera Sempa, "Police halts UYD seminar," *Njuba Times*, July 25, 1998.

[203]James Mujuni, "DP rally blocked in Mbarara," *New Vision*, July 22, 1998.

[204]Adams Wamakesi and Charles F. Guluma, "Police Disperse Mbale UPC Meet," *Monitor*, July 27, 1998.

activities here to confuse our people but he can't listen."[205] The FHRI seminar was
allowed to proceed after it was explained to the RDC that it was sponsored by
FHRI which is directed by Livingstone Sewanyana, not FAD which is directed by
Anthony Ssekweyama.[206]

According to the government-owned *New Vision*, an August 9, 1998, seminar
organized by former presidential candidate and president of the opposition Justice
Forum, Kibirige Mayanja, to address the topic of "Poverty Alleviation in Uganda:
A Review of the Leader/Led Relationship," was prevented from taking place by
armed policemen. The newspaper reported that the decision to stop the seminar
was taken by the Iganga district authorities.[207]

Opposition Politician Chapaa Arrested

Karuhanga Chapaa, chair of the National Democrats Forum, was arrested at
his office in Kampala on December 17, 1998, by four plainclothes police officers,
and taken to Kampala police station for questioning. After being kept overnight
in detention, Chapaa was charged with sedition in relation to comments he
reportedly made at a December 13, 1998, political rally at Nateete sponsored by
member of parliament Ken Lukyamuzi. The charges are based on a report
published in the *Crusader* newspaper, entitled "Museveni worse than Amin,
Obote—Chapaa," which claimed that Chapaa had stated at the rally that "Amin and
Obote were dictators but they were not thieves. Museveni is a dictator and a thief,"
"Museveni is a hardened thief," "Now many Banyankore feel ashamed because
Museveni is spoiling their name," and "This movement is already dead and we
should bury it."[208] In a December 15 letter to the *Crusader*, Chapaa denied making
the statements and asked for a correction, stating that he had only said that
Museveni's regime was dictatorial and full of corrupt leaders.[209] The editor of the
Crusader newspaper, George Lugalambi, was arrested at the same time as Chapaa,
and charged with "promoting sectarianism" in regards to an unrelated article (see

---

[205]Mukiibi Sserwanga, "Armed RDC storms scribes workshop," *Njuba Times*, July 30,
1998.

[206]Livingstone Sewanyana, executive director of FHRI, confirmed in an interview with
Human Rights Watch that the RDC had interrupted the meeting, but believed that the RDC
had confused him with Henry Sewanyana, the former FAD director, and not Anthony
Ssekweyama, the current FAD director. Human Rights Watch interview with Livingstone
Sewanyana, Harare, Zimbabwe, August 6, 1998.

[207]Daniel Saire, "Mayanja to Mourn," *New Vision*, August 10, 1998.

[208]"Museveni worse than Amin, Obote—Chapaa," *Crusader*, December 15, 1998.

[209]Letter to the Editor of Crusader Newspaper from Karuhanga Chapaa, dated
December 15, 1998.

below). Chapaa was released on bail of 500,000 shillings (approximately U.S. $500), two sureties of 10 million shillings each (approximately U.S. $10,000 each), and was required to surrender his passport.[210]

Uganda includes among its definition of sedition the uttering of any words with the intent "to bring into hatred or contempt or to excite disaffection against the person of the President, the Government as by law established or the Constitution," an offence punishable by a five-year jail sentence and a fine.[211] While "promoting sectarianism" is not defined in the penal code as a criminal offense, it is an act of sedition to "promote feelings of ill-will and hostility, religious animosity or communal ill-feeling among any body or group of persons.[212] Chapaa was convicted of sedition on June 28, 1999, and ordered to pay a 50,000 shilling (approximately U.S. $50 fine). He informed Human Rights Watch that he plans to appeal the sentence.

On December 26, 1998, Chapaa received a letter from the resident district commissioner of Bushenyi, entitled "Warning on illegal political activities and defamatory/treasonable utterances." Claiming that Chapaa was "carrying out illegal political activities in Bushenyi district," and had attended an "illegal political rally at Bitereko ... in which you uttered defamatory words against the President [and] also made treasonable utterances against the Government of the Republic of Uganda," the letter warned Chapaa "to stop illegal political activities." In addition to warning Chapaa not to violate articles 269, 73, and 270 of the constitution, the letter also told Chapaa to desist from distributing party cards, "which is an illegal act." The letter justified the warning as appropriate under the RDC's capacity as chair of the district security committee, because "your utterances have caused disharmony and are likely to destabilise the District in terms of Security."[213] Chapaa responded that he had not made a statement at Bitereko, but had merely driven around the region to wave to his supporters: "On that fateful day of 26 December 1998, I just drove around in my constituency of Ruhinda to wave to my supporters, I did not even disembark from my car."[214]

---

[210]Bail Bond, Uganda v. Karuhanga Chapaa, dated December 18, 1998.

[211]Uganda Penal Code (1984 revised edition), Sections 41 and 42.

[212]Uganda Penal Code, Section 41(1)(e).

[213]Letter of Drani Dradriga, Resident District Commissioner, Bushenyi district, to Karuhanga Chapaa, dated January 4, 1999.

[214]Fax from Karahunga Chapaa to Human Rights Watch, dated January 13, 1998.

Member of Parliament Wasswa Lule Arrested

Wasswa Lule, a member of parliament for Rubaga North, describes his arrest at his home on January 6, 1999:

> I was sitting down to have supper at about 8:15 p.m. on Wednesday 6th January, 1999. I was at my residence in Lugujja, Makamba zone when two plain clothes policemen requested to see me. They were accompanied by a large contingent of uniformed policemen armed with sub-machine guns which appeared to be Kalasnikov AK 47's. I am made to understand that they were up to thirty in number. I was shown a handwritten document with the narrative "proceed to Lungujja and arrest Hon. Wasswa Lule."[215]

Lule was taken to the Kampala central police station where he was interrogated about statements allegedly made at a Ramadan seminar organized by the Uganda Muslim Youth Assembly, attributed to him in a *Monitor* newspaper article of January 4, 1999, entitled "Time to probe Museveni—MP." According to the *Monitor* article, Lule said that it had become necessary to investigate President Museveni personally for corruption because others close to the president, including the president's brother, had been implicated in corruption. Lule also reportedly claimed that he had been fired from his position as deputy inspector general of government so corrupt officials could steal Uganda's wealth.[216] Lule was alleged to have made the statements when the Museveni administration was engulfed in corruption allegations which had led to the resignations of President Museveni's brother, Major General Salim Saleh and Minister of State for Privatization Matthew Rukikaire.

Lule was detained until about 2 a.m. According to the *Monitor*, police spokesman Bob Ngobi stated that Lule "was not under arrest but was wanted for interrogation over utterances [which] attacked the person of the president, and are likely to raise disaffection against the person of the president and government of Uganda; an offence under the penal code."[217] Under Uganda's penal code, "uttering any words with [an] intention" "to bring into hatred or contempt or to excite disaffection against the person of the President [or] the Government" is

---

[215]Fax from Wasswa Lule, member of parliament (Rubuga North), to Human Rights Watch dated January 7, 1999.

[216]Ssemujju Ibrahim Nganda, "Time to probe Museveni—MP," *Monitor*, January 4, 1999.

[217]"MP Lule arrested," *Monitor*, January 7, 1999.

considered sedition and can lead to a five-year maximum prison term.[218] Shortly before his arrest, Lule was criticized by President Museveni's wife for calling for a corruption investigation of the president.[219]

Arrest of FAD Officials in Moyo

On January 16, 1999, three Foundation for African Development officials attempted to organize a training session on civic education in Moyo, a town in the West Nile region of Uganda, near the Sudanese border. Soon after the seminar began with opening remarks at about 11:30 a.m., a police officer entered the seminar room and requested to see the "leader of the team that came from Kampala." Constantine Embatia and Hellen Acam, both FAD officials, identified themselves and were informed that the district police commander (DPC) wanted to see them.

When the two FAD officials arrived at the office of the DPC, they were informed by a police officer that the Moyo resident district commissioner wanted to see them at 2:30 p.m. and that they should remain at the police station until that time. According to a statement by one of the FAD officials obtained by Human Rights Watch, a vehicle soon left the station with police to disperse the seminar:

> At about 12:45 p.m., while we were at the police station, I saw six armed men board a police pick-up and drive out of the station.
>
> This vehicle...went to the venue of the training. While at the [Moyo Technical Institute], the armed police men took position around the hall and at the doors while the rest stormed the hall. The commander ordered everybody to stand up and leave everything.... The calm and peaceful participants obeyed the orders. [The policemen] collected the items which were on the desks and searched the cavera [sic] which was containing the balance of stationery and money which was for facilitating the training. The participants were ordered to leave the hall and the two police officers were last to come [out] after seeing everybody out.[220]

Ally Ssali, a third FAD official who had remained at the seminar, was taken to the police station by police after the dispersal of the seminar.

---

[218]Uganda Penal Code, Sections 41 and 42.

[219]Ibid.

[220]Embatia Constantine, "Report of What Happened to us in Moyo," undated.

The three FAD officials were allowed to leave the police station for lunch, and then returned to wait in vain for the Commissioner. At about 3:15 p.m., one of the FAD officials asked to see him and was brought to his office. According to the FAD official, the Commissioner "faked ignorance of what was going on." The FAD official returned to the police station with no explanation of the reason for their detention and the disruption of the seminar.

At about 5 p.m., the district police commissioner called the three FAD officials into his office and informed them that he had just returned from a meeting with the RDC and the district security committee and was under instructions to detain the three FAD officials in police cells until 9:30 a.m. the next day. Later than night, the FAD officials inquired to a police officer whether they had been officially booked in, because they wanted to ensure that their detention was recorded. The duty officer informed them that they had not been recorded in the lock-up record, and the three FAD officials argued with the station commander that their detention was improper because the police had not recorded the detention and was refusing to state the grounds for the detention as required by Ugandan law. According to the FAD officials, the station commander replied that he had been instructed to keep the three in safe custody "until further instructions are received from higher authorities." However, the officer later relented, and allowed the three officials to return to their hotel after confiscating their documents and some other property, and ordering them to report to the police station early the next morning.

Soon after their return to the hotel, the district police commissioner arrived there and ordered the three to return to the police station. At 10 a.m. the next day, after spending the night in police custody, the police recorded statements of two of the FAD officials. Shortly after 11 a.m., the three FAD officials were taken to the office of the RDC, were they were questioned by the District Security Committee for about an hour about FAD activities. At the end of the meeting, the FAD officials were asked to apologize for coming to the district without permission and holding an unlawful assembly. The FAD officials refused to apologize, arguing that there were no legal grounds for this request. The three were then told to return to the police station while the District Security Committee deliberated on how to proceed.

When the district police commissioner returned to the police station, he continued to demand a written apology from the FAD officials. According to the FAD officials, the commissioner insisted on the apology letter as a condition of release, telling Constantine Embatia that "you will be released on the condition that you write an apology letter condemning your activities in the district and apologizing for it." The commissioner returned again at about 2:45 p.m., asking Embatia if she had finished her apology letter. Embatia protested that she was being coerced to write the apology letter, to which the DPC replied that the letter was the condition for their release and that the choice was entirely up to her. After consulting with her colleagues, Embatia decided to write the letter in order to obtain their release. The three were released at about 3:45 p.m. on January 17, approximately twenty-eight hours after their original arrest.

Many of the statements attributed to local officials by the FAD organizers suggest that the seminar was broken up for political reasons. A local FAD organizer informed the organization's officials that the district council chairperson had described the FAD seminar as a multiparty meeting intended to cause disruption in the district, and that the meeting should be prevented from taking place. According to the FAD organizers, the policeman who first arrived at the seminar told them: "You people of FAD, wherever you go you always cause problems and confusion, you caused problems for our people in Tororo [and] Mbarara and now you want to put us in trouble."[221]

Harassment of NDF Activist

On April 19, 1999, Daudi Kagambirwe, a member of the National Democrats Forum (NDF), handed out official NDF documents at the end of a district meeting of the Uganda National Students Association, of which he was the acting district chairperson. On April 21, the district internal security officer (DISO) told Kagambirwe that his NDF activities were "improper and illegal." On May 5, 1999, Kagambirwe was arrested by a plainclothes security operative, who told him that he was required to give a statement to the police. He was taken to Kabale police station, and was kept in custody from the time of his arrest at 4 p.m. until 9 a.m. the next morning. When he left the station, Kagambirwe heard the DISO talking to a police officer, stating that Kagambirwe was a member of the NDF, "a political wing of the ADF [rebel group] and [he] will have to explain over this." He was required to return to the police station on May 8 to answer further questions about his membership in the NDF.[222]

Local Official Harassed after FAD Seminar

On April 26, 1999, the Foundation for African Development organized a workshop on "Human Rights in the Community" in Mpingi District. The workshop was attended by eighty-one community members, including local council leaders and police officials, and featured two presentations by FAD officials as well as a presentation on the role of the community in promoting human rights by a

---

[221]Ibid.
[222]Signed Statement of Daudi Kagambirwe, dated 8 May 1999.

local police officer. According to a signed statement by FAD officials to Human Rights Watch, local council chairperson Paul Ssemwanga Sooka was approached by the police officer in charge of the Kabulassoke police station, Francis Asiimwe, and two officers of the Internal Security Organization (ISO) after the completion of the seminar. The police and ISO officers claimed that the workshop was illegal, and asked the council chairperson why he believed he had the power to bring FAD workshops to the area. According to the FAD statement, the officials told the chairperson "never to offer [a] platform to FAD officials in that kind of a forum," and extorted money from him after threatening to forward the matter to higher authorities.[223]

Detention and Questioning of NDF Member

At about 3 p.m. on June 11, 1999, Ahimbisibwe Ponsiano, a former UPDF soldier who joined the National Democrats Forum (NDF), was arrested by two men and a woman in civilian clothes at a private business in Nakulabye, a suburb of Kampala. The trio entered the private business, asked for Ponsiano by name, and then asked him to accompany them. He was taken to a private house which was guarded by UPDF soldiers in Kabowa, another suburb of Kampala. At about 9 p.m., Lieutenant Colonel John Mugisha, the apparent owner of the house, arrived and started to question Ponsiano. Mugisha first asked Ponsiano what he had been doing since his retirement from the UPDF, but rapidly focused his questions on Ponsiano's membership in the NDF and the activities of the NDF and its chairperson, Karuhanga K. Chapaa.

After the questioning ended and Mugisha left the room to make a telephone call, Ponsiano was taken to his home by two armed men. The two men searched Ponsiano's home, and then took him to another home in Bukoto, a suburb of Kampala, where he was further questioned by UPDF officers, including Lieutenant Colonel Kasaijia, the owner of the house. The officers questioned Ponsiano about his relatives in Mbarara district who belong to the NDF, Ponsiano's meetings with Chapaa, and "safe houses" where Chapaa conducts meetings. The officers then proceeded to ask why the NDF is recruiting UPDF veterans, to which Ponsiano replied that all Ugandans were welcome in the NDF. Finally, the officers asked Ponsiano about Chapaa's relationships with other opposition politicians, including Members of Parliament Wasswa Lule, Ken Lukyamuzi, and Aggrey Awori.

---

[223]Aloyius Ssali, "Harassment after a Foundation for African Development (FAD) Training Workshop Organized at Kabulassoke-Gomba, in Mpigi District, on Monday, 26th April, 1999," dated May 5, 1999.

After the interrogation ended at about midnight, Ponsiano was told to sleep at the house. In the morning, he was taken to Katwe police station and told to write a statement about his NDF activities. Shortly afterwards, some men whom Ponsiano believed belonged to a security organization arrived and told the police to release Ponsiano. Ponsiano was released, but was required to report to the police station on a regular basis afterwards.[224]

The Ban on Party Conferences and Freedom of Association and Assembly

Movement supporters accuse political parties of lacking internal democracy; they claim that the parties continue to be run by the same politicians who founded the parties at the time of Uganda's independence. However, the very restrictions put in place by article 269 perpetuate these internal characteristics, in effect freezing the leadership and structures of the political parties in time. Indeed, Minister of State for Justice and Constitutional Affairs Emmanuel Kirenga issued a strong warning when the DP tried to convene a party conference to change the party's leadership, stating that he would not hesitate to take action against them if the proscribed conference was convened.[225] Thus, President Museveni continues to describe the UPC of being the party of Milton Obote—a powerful message in a country which was brutalized during Obote's reign—while at the same time denying the UPC the opportunity to call a delegates' conference to reform its leadership. Patrick Mwondha, the secretary of the interim executive council of the UPC, a faction of the UPC which no longer recognizes Milton Obote as the leader of the UPC, described this:

> Article 269 stipulates that parties cannot hold delegates' conferences. Our party constitution says that the delegates' conference elects the leadership of the party, so we are caught between the party constitution and the national constitution. We would have to break the law to hold a delegates' conference. Even amending our constitution requires a delegates' conference.[226]

---

[224]Signed statement of Ahimbisibwe Ponsiano, dated June 14, 1999; letter of Columban Oloka, Secretary-General of NDF Youth League, to Human Rights Watch, dated June 15, 1999.

[225]Paul Kaddu, "Democratic Party Warned on Conference," *New Vision*, October 17, 1997.

[226]Human Rights Watch interview with Patrick Mwondha, Secretary, Interim Executive Committee, Uganda People's Congress, Kampala, May 9, 1998.

The view that the political restrictions under the movement system limit the ability of the UPC and other parties to institute democratic reforms was echoed by outgoing U.S. Ambassador Michael Southwick, who stated in an interview in 1997: "I am amazed that [Obote] still generates headlines and even leads a political party. But I would not necessarily blame the UPC because it is not operating under free conditions. If it were, we would probably see a much different UPC."[227] John Ssenkumba, a researcher at Makerere University's Centre for Basic Research, argues that the ban on delegate conferences is one of the tools used by the NRM to ensure their own continuation in power:

> To rejuvenate themselves, parties need to restructure themselves, something practically impossible with the present ban. By keeping the country unripe for pluralism, and ensuring unconducive conditions for the emergence of any non-NRM alternative, the NRM has politically ensured some tentative political invincibility.[228]

The Proposed Political Organizations Bill

Article 72 of the Ugandan constitution requires parliament to adopt legislation to govern the financing and functioning of political parties.[229] In December 1998, the Political Organizations Bill (1998), a bill to strictly regulate the conduct and organization of political parties, was tabled in parliament by the minister of justice and constitutional affairs. However, as discussed below, the government has repeatedly withdrawn the bill, preferring for the moment to allow the more stringent restrictions of article 269 of the constitution to remain in force.

Although some of the requirements set out in the bill appear to be designed to ensure that political parties adhere to certain minimum democratic standards, the vagueness of many of the proposed regulations would give the NRM-controlled government tremendous power to control political parties. The regulations contained in the Political Parties Organizations Bill place a severe burden on the ability of political organizations in Uganda to operate freely and effectively. When looked at in its entirety, the political organizations bill raises many concerns. Like article 269, the Political Parties Bill will allow the NRM administration to allow

---

[227]Ofwono Opondo, "U.S. warns Uganda over referendum," *Sunday Vision*, July 20, 1997, p.1.

[228]John Ssenkumba, "NRM Politics, Political Parties and the Demobilization of Organized Political Forces," (March 1997), p. 13.

[229]Uganda Constitution (1995), Article 72.

political parties to exist in name, but to regulate their activities so restrictively that they are effectively deprived of their ability to organize.

In Uganda's post-independence history, some political parties have at times operated in an undemocratic and unconstitutional manner, and the Ugandan government may have a legitimate interest in preventing such abuses in the future. The Ugandan government may legitimately outlaw and punish illegal or unconstitutional activities by political parties, like incitement to violence. But the government cannot use its concerns about such activities to impose an overbroad and arbitrary ban which encompasses the internationally protected activities of political parties.

The Exclusion of the NRM "Movement" Structures from Regulation

One of the most fundamental concerns about the Political Organizations Bill is that it excludes the movement political system and the organs created under the movement political system from its regulations (Section 3(2)(a)). Thus, while political parties are rigidly controlled by the regulations in the Bill, the former NRM structures—transformed into "movement" structures—are allowed to continue functioning without regulation. The NRM's "movement" structures are to be privileged in the same way that the NRM structures currently benefit from their exclusion from the political restrictions of article 269 of the Constitution. This blatant discriminatory application of the regulations is inconsistent with international standards.

All political organizations, including the amorphous movement structures, if they are regulated at all, should be regulated in a nondiscriminatory manner. Candidates running for public office should be required to abide by the same set of rules governing financing, campaigning and other matters, regardless of their political affiliation (including membership in the ruling "movement"). Candidates for public office, whether members of political parties or of the "movement," should have equal access to government funding, as well as equal right to fundraise.

Onerous Restrictions on the Establishment of Political Parties

The Political Organizations Bill also restricts the establishment of political parties. Such limitations should be proportional to the legitimate aims advanced, and should not be so onerous as to effectively undermine freedom of association. Some of the proposed requirements placed upon the registration of political parties and their conduct are onerous and arbitrary. Even those that would be acceptable under international standards if applied uniformly to all political parties and similar organizations are discriminatory because NRM structures are exempt.

Section 6 of the proposed bill prohibits the formation of political organizations whose membership is based on "sex, race, color, ethnic, birth, creed or religion or other similar division," as well as parties "which use words, slogans or symbols which could arouse" such divisions, and parties which do not have a national character. Some of these proposed restrictions are vague and could easily be abused by an administration hostile to opposition political parties. The proposed prohibition on the use of speech which could arouse divisions is overly broad. For example, several Buganda parliamentarians raised concerns about the proposed land bill in early 1998, and it would seem that the raising of such regional concerns could fall under the ambit of section 6, prohibiting the use of "words" which could arouse "division."[230] Section 6 of the bill is inconsistent with the right to freedom of speech contained in the ICCPR.

Under section 7, political parties would be required to pay a nonrefundable fee of two million shillings (approximately U.S. $2,000) to obtain registration, a substantial amount by Ugandan standards. Parties would need to deposit with the electoral commission copies of their constitution and a list of founding members in at least one third of districts of Uganda to obtain registration (section 9). The proposed requirement of having founding members in at least one third of the forty-five districts establishes a high threshold, given Uganda's rudimentary communications and infrastructure system. This proposed requirement would severely limit the formation of new democratic institutions in Uganda. In effect, these requirements will stifle the emergence of new political parties which tend to start with a small regional or urban base, since such incipient organizations will most likely not be able to attract founding members in one-third of Uganda's districts.

The requirement that each political party have a "national" character (Section 6) is also problematic. In many countries, regional parties compete effectively for power. While it is legitimate for government to restrict some of the disruptive activities sometimes associated with ethnic, religious or regionally based parties—such as criminal provisions punishing political violence—a complete ban on parties which do not have a national character is too broad a measure to achieve such a goal.

The Exclusion of Certain Groups from Political Activities

Article 23 of the Political Organizations Bill excludes all members of the army (UPDF), the Uganda Police Force, the Uganda Prisons Service, as well as

---

[230]In fact, Buganda activists were restricted in challenging the land bill, as discussed in this report.

"public officers" (a term not defined in the bill), traditional rulers, and cultural leaders[231] from participation in a wide variety of political activities. Members of these groups cannot be founders or members of political organizations, are not eligible to hold office in a political organization, "speak in public or publish anything involving matters of political organisation controversy," and cannot engage in canvassing in support of candidates sponsored by political parties.

Many countries ban members of the armed forces and the police force from politics, so political restrictions placed on these groups may be legally more acceptable than those placed on other groups. While there are grounds in international law for restrictions on the freedom of association of members of the armed forces and the police—such restrictions are specifically envisioned by Article 22 of the ICCPR[232]—these restrictions should be carefully tailored and be applied without discrimination.

The Political Parties Bill does not exclude members of the armed forces and the police from *politics*: it merely excludes them from *opposition political party politics*. Active UPDF officers have participated in politics since the coming to power of the NRA in 1986. President Museveni himself, a number of his cabinet ministers, as well as a significant number of parliamentarians and local council members at all levels, are officers in the UPDF. The Political Organizations Bill does not restrict politically active UPDF and police officers from engaging in national or local politics in their individual capacity or under the umbrella of the NRM "movement," a distinction which could be viewed as arbitrary.

The exclusion of members of the Uganda Prisons Service, public officers, and traditional and cultural leaders from political activities is arbitrary under international norms, as these groups are not traditionally barred from political participation. In fact, the exclusion of all members of the public administration from the enjoyment of freedom of association was specifically rejected during the

---

[231]Defined in the bill as "a king or similar traditional leader or cultural leader by whatever name called, who derives allegiance from the fact of birth or descent in accordance with the customs, traditions, usage or consent of the people led by that traditional or cultural leader." Section 3(1).

[232]ICCPR Art. 22(2): "This article shall not prevent the imposition of lawful restrictions on members of the armed forces and of the police" See also Nowak, *CCPR Commentary*, p 397: "[T]he special status and responsibility of the military and police represents an additional purpose for interference, which permits much farther-reaching restrictions on the right of association for members of these two institutions. For instance, many States restrict the political activities of the police and the military in order to prevent the armed forces from impermissibly meddling in the political affairs of the civilian constitutional organs."

debates leading up to the adoption of article 22 of the ICCPR, and the exclusion of persons other than military or police officers from freedom of association rights must therefore be considered to fall outside the specific language of the article.[233]

In addition, the prohibitions placed on speech (including publication) for all groups who have their political activities restricted is overly broad. The limitation envisioned in article 22 of the ICCPR is clearly limited to restrictions on freedom of association, and similar restrictions are not envisioned under the rights of freedom of speech or assembly.

Continuing Restrictions on the Activities of Political Parties

Although it purports to regulate, not repress, political parties, the draft Political Organizations Bill retains many of the restrictions on political party activity previously contained in Article 269 of the Uganda constitution.[234] Section 24(a) of the Political Organizations Bill states that under the movement system, "no political organisation and no person on behalf of a political organisation shall sponsor or offer a platform to or in any way campaign for or against a candidate in any presidential or parliamentary election or any other election," a restriction similar to that contained in article 269(d) of the constitution. Candidates for public office are also banned from using "any symbol, slogan, colour or name identifying any political organisation for the purpose of campaigning for or against any candidate" in an election (Section 24(b)).

These limitations on the activities of political parties and their candidates strike at the very heart of political party activities. The Political Organizations Bill itself defines a political party as "a political organisation the objects of which include the sponsoring of, or offering a platform to, candidates for election to a political office and participation in the governance of Uganda at all levels," only to ban political parties from engaging in exactly those activities. It appears this prohibition covers political rallies during election periods as well.

In addition to requiring political parties to notify the local police commander seventy-two hours before holding any meeting, the proposed legislation prohibits political parties from holding meetings in the same place at the same time (Section 22(2)). While notice requirements are justifiable under international law, the frequent abuse of such provisions to interrupt and disperse political events under

---

[233]Nowak, *CCPR Commentary*, p. 397.

[234]The Uganda constitution specifically envisions that article 269 will be superseded by legislation, limiting the operation of article 269, "until Parliament makes laws regulating the activities of political organisations."

the current system (as documented here) argues for a reformed notification scheme in order to prevent such arbitrary interferences.

The minister in charge of elections and referenda is given wide-ranging powers under the bill to further regulate political organizations, although the approval of parliament is necessary. In particular, the bill allows the minister, with the approval of parliament, to adopt regulations regarding "the opening of branch offices, holding of delegates' conferences, public rallies and any other activities of political organisations as may be reasonably necessary to prevent interference with the operation of the movement political system when that system is in existence in Uganda," (Section 32(2)(a)), mirroring the restrictions currently contained in Article 269 of the Constitution. Because of the frequent hostility shown by the NRM administration to opposition political parties, the appointment of an NRM minister to regulate these political parties could lead to many further restrictions on political organizations. In order to avoid the danger of further arbitrary or abusive restrictions on political organizations, it would be better to appoint an independent and impartial body to oversee the regulation of political organizations. This position is shared by the Uganda Human Rights Commission, which states that "no Minister should in any way control the operation of political parties or political organizations. An independent authority should be vested with this responsibility."[235]

The Referendum on Political Parties in the Year 2000

The Ugandan constitution grants the Ugandan people the right to choose a political system of their choice through "free and fair elections or referenda."[236] The electorate may choose between the movement political system or the multiparty system, both defined in the constitution, or any other "democratic and representative political system."

The constitution states that the first elections for president, parliament, and local government will be held under the movement system, but requires the holding of a referendum in the fourth year] of the first term of parliament "to determine the political system the people of Uganda wish to adopt."[237] The referendum and other provisions act requires the Electoral Commission to set a date between June 3 and July 2, 2000, for the referendum. [238] After this initial referendum, it remains

---

[235]Uganda Human Rights Commission, Views on the Political Organisations Bill (undated).

[236]Uganda Constitution (1995), article 69(1).

[237]Ibid., article 271(1) and (3).

[238]Referendum and Other Provisions Act, Act No. 2 of 1999, section 26.

possible to change the political system in the future either by referendum or by elections if certain conditions are met.[239]

The Adoption of the Referendum Act

The Referendum and Other Provisions Act was adopted amid controversy on July 2, 1999, the constitutional deadline for the adoption of the legislation. Along with opposition political parties and the media, the Ugandan Law Society protested that the legislation was scarcely debated and had been rushed through parliament without a quorum:

> The Society would like to express its gravest concern over the way the Referendum and Other Provisions Bill was debated in a record 24 hours.... This is such an important piece of legislation to the citizens because it will lead to the determination of the political arena of this country. Not giving it thorough surgery was a disservice to the citizens and we call upon the legislature which is answerable to its electorate to provide a satisfactory answer to such an act. To add to this injury, the bill was debated when there was no quorum.[240]

The constitution envisioned that the Ugandan government would adopt two pieces of legislation: referendum legislation to regulate the holding of the referendum, and political organizations legislation to regulate the functioning of political parties. For political parties to freely campaign during the referendum period, however, it was necessary to pass the political organizations bill prior to the beginning of the referendum campaign period. While the political organizations bill was introduced to parliament long before the referendum bill, the government chose to withdraw this bill from parliament just shortly before passage of the referendum and other provisions act. Through this maneuver, the NRM has succeeded in ensuring that political parties will continue to be handicapped by the restrictions of article 269 of the constitution during the referendum campaign period. Thus, there will be no level playing field for opposition political parties during the referendum campaign period.

The NRM's manipulation of the legal framework for the referendum led to a rejection of the referendum by all six major opposition political organizations in

---

[239]These conditions are contained in article 74 of the Constitution.

[240]Press Conference called by the Uganda Law Society, July 4, 1999. See also, Robert Mukasa and Ted Nannozi, "Referendum Bill Dragged Through," *Monitor*, July 2, 1999; Conrad Nkutu, ""Is There No Shame in the Movement?," *New Vision*, July 4, 1999.

Uganda—the DP, UPC, Free Movement, Conservative Party, National Democrats Forum, and the Justice Forum. In a joint statement, the opposition political organizations declared that they would not take part in the referendum:

> Given the fact that the Movement government has taken the extreme position of denying political parties a legitimate legal framework by withdrawing the Political Organizations Bill and passing an unfair Referendum Bill, the Political Parties and civic organizations find themselves locked out of the referendum contest and have no option but to reject the Referendum Bill and the subsequent referendum exercise.[241]

The Uganda Law Society was equally critical of the withdrawal of the political parties bill, stating that "the ground level is not even" and that "the referendum may not be free and fair."[242]

Continuing Restrictions during the Referendum Period

The constitution does allow some limited debate on the future political system, stating that in the year prior to the referendum, "*any person* shall be free to canvass for public support for a political system of his or her choice."[243] The granting of this right to canvass to individuals was deliberate. Parties continue to be prohibited from holding public rallies during the run-up to the referendum, so organized opposition to a vote for the movement system is effectively handicapped, while the NRM can mobilize its supporters through the state-sponsored movement structures.

Because article 269 of the constitution remains in force, opposition political parties are deprived of the opportunity to mount an effective campaign in the referendum. As noted, article 269 prohibits political parties from opening or operating branch offices, holding delegates' conferences, holding public rallies, sponsoring candidates for elections, or engaging in any activities "that may interfere with the movement political system."

The referendum act requires each "side" to the referendum to form a national referendum committee whose duties will include "to organize the canvassing for its side, and to appoint agents for the purpose of canvassing." Such committees cannot be considered a substitute for the opposition political parties. Political parties should not be required to form a unified referendum committee but should

---

[241]Press Release, "Political Parties Reject the Referendum," July 2, 1999.
[242]Press Conference called by the Uganda Law Society, July 4, 1999.
[243]Ibid., Article 271 (3) (emphasis added).

rather be allowed to canvass for themselves in a referendum which is fundamentally about their survival.

The referendum act does allow "any agent ... either alone or in common with others" to publish canvassing materials such as books, pamphlets, leaflets, or posters.[244] However, when using the private electronic media during canvassing, agents are prohibited from making false or reckless statements, malicious statements, statements containing sectarian words or allusions, abusive, insulting or derogatory statements, exaggerations, caricatures, or words of ridicule, or using derisive or mudslinging words.[245] These prohibitions on forms of speech are overly broad and vague, and inconsistent with freedom of speech standards. Their broad and vague nature could sanction the suppression of speech which falls within the ambit of protected speech. As with the draft political organizations bill, the minister responsible for elections can make additional regulations regulating the canvassing process, with the approval of parliament. Because of the long history of hostility of pro-NRM ministers towards opposition political parties, such powers should lie with an independent and impartial body.

The Rejection of the Referendum by the Opposition

With the exception of a those closely identified with the NRM and the movement system, few persons interviewed by Human Rights Watch believed that the referendum on political parties could be free and fair in light of the movement's domination of the political arena through discriminatory laws. Paul Ssemogerere, president of the Democratic Party and the main contender against Museveni in the 1996 presidential elections, stated to Human Rights Watch:

> There cannot be a fair referendum in Uganda. We are against it on principle. The process is being rigged in advance. I know what I went through as a presidential candidate and the movement will fight hard. The movement will use government structures extensively during this time. The Movement Act will also be used to prepare the ground. They will continue to demonize the parties, calling them Kony's and Obote's allies. The movement is not a system, it is a political organization. The country and the international community are being deceived. The vote

---

[244] The Referendum and Other Provisions Act, No. 2 of 1999, section 21(2).
[245] Ibid, section 21(5).

is absolutely about a one-party state. I will not participate in this charade, even if I remain alone.[246]

In commenting on the upcoming referendum, a member of the electoral commission charged with organizing and monitoring elections said:

I don't think we can have a fair referendum. You cannot have twelve years of a movement system and then expect one year [of campaigning] to change things. People on the ground do not understand the political system and vote for personalities. They will vote for movement because they like Museveni. How do you phrase a question on which people are allowed to vote? ... It will not be a fair referendum.[247]

Advocates of pluralism and opposition politicians in Uganda expressed similar skepticism about the referendum, and the six main opposition parties have publicly called upon their supporters to boycott the referendum. Law Professor Frederick Jjuuko, Chair of the Freedom Movement, a recently formed group advocating a speedy return to political pluralism in Uganda, explained his opposition to the referendum:

I do not think that there can be a fair referendum on the political system in Uganda, and we intend to call for a boycott of the referendum. It is not designed to be conducted in good faith to determine the will of the people on the movement system, but rather to perpetuate the movement into perpetuity.

There are a number of reasons why the referendum cannot be fair. The movement has been on the scene for a long time and has developed a virtual monopoly on ideas, and they have political schools called chaka-mchaka which they combine with military training to spread their messages. The parties have not been able to do this, and there has been a systematic attempt to kill the political parties. It is contradictory to suppress the parties for all these years and then expect them to put on a

---

[246]Human Rights Watch interview with Paul Ssemogerere, President, Democratic Party, Mengo, May 7, 1998.

[247]Human Rights Watch interview with Robert Kitariko, member, Uganda Electoral Commission, Kampala, May 7, 1998. Kitariko has in the past been a high-ranking member of the Democratic Party.

campaign equal to the movement which has access to state resources. The odds are all against the political parties.[248]

Cecilia Ogwal, leader of the influential Interim Executive Council of the UPC, has similarly called for a boycott of the referendum, calling it a "death trap for the future."[249] Her colleague, Patrick Mwondha of the UPC, suggested that the referendum was the culmination of a concerted campaign to destroy political parties in Uganda:

> Museveni himself calls us enemies. What do you do to an enemy? That shows you the mentality of the man. He does not see us as opponents or legitimate alternatives to himself. Museveni has not allowed the opposition, he has put up with it—there is a big difference. We started with an administrative ban which was enforced furiously. Then came article 269 in the constitution, and it is now being translated into the Political Organizations Bill. The referendum will seal everything.[250]

Cardinal Emmanuel Wamala, leader of Uganda's influential Catholic Church, also expressed his opposition to the proposed referendum during his 1998 Christmas address, stating that the referendum would infringe fundamental human rights.[251] Similarly, in his Idd-El Fitir address marking the end of the Muslim holy month of Ramadan, Sheikh Mukasa, leader of the largest Muslim community in Uganda, urged the Ugandan government to amend the constitution and abandon the referendum, stating that the referendum would lead to a denial of the right to associate freely.[252]

According to Winnie Byanyima, a member of parliament and an outspoken movement supporter, the real issue behind the referendum for movement supporters is different:

---

[248]Human Rights Watch interview with Frederick Jjuuko, Makerere University law professor, Kampala, April 14, 1998.

[249]Levi Ochieng, "We will boycott referendum, pledge parties," *East African*, May 4-10, 1998, p.2.

[250]Human Rights Watch interview with Patrick Mwondha, Secretary of the Interim Executive Committee, Uganda People's Congress, Kampala, May 9, 1998.

[251]"Catholic Church Leader Opposes Referendum on Political Systems," *New Vision*, December 27, 1998.

[252]"Kibuli Mufti Rejects Referendum on Parties," *New Vision*, January 18, 1998.

The transition is coming to an end and some people do not want to recognize this. Those in power and those who are gaining from the system of the day fear change. I sought to define the movement as a transitional arrangement [at the constituent assembly debates] and was branded a traitor, a multipartyist. It was clear that there were two camps: the larger saying that the movement is an alternative form of government and our smaller group which said that we could not infringe those rights forever. There has to be a referendum every five years, but I never wanted this. It is a problem of handing over power, it is always a problem in Africa. Even after doing very well, it is always a problem to democratize.[253]

The suggestion that movement leaders are aiming to entrench themselves in power is born out by frequent statements by movement leaders at rallies that the movement system will remain in power in Uganda. For example, at a May 3, 1998, rally in Gulu Prime Minister Kintu Musoke told the crowd:

The system is now permanent, so come in and struggle for power and not from outside. Come on the boat which is broad-based.... The NRM system is like a basket full of everything and even if you kick it, it cannot fall. It will be stable and will be for good.[254]

Similar statements are often made by government representatives such as resident district commissioners. For example, the RDC of Mukono, Peter Kalagala, told local residents that the movement was here to stay and could not be ousted: "Whether you like it or not, the Movement system came to stay like the water hyacinth, so just leave it alone."[255]

---

[253]Human Rights Watch interview with Winnie Byanyima MP (Mbarara district), Kampala, April 12, 1998.

[254]Statements of Prime Minister Kintu Misoke at May 3, 1998 Gulu rally.

[255]Mike Musisi-Musoke, "NRM is like *kiddo*—RDC," *Monitor*, April 28, 1998, p.7. The reference to the water hyacinth (kiddo) alludes to the water hyacinth plant which was introduced in Uganda's Lake Victoria years ago and has now become so overgrown that it is choking the lake of oxygen and killing the fish. It is considered virtually impossible to remove.

The Referendum and International Standards

Referenda are an important way in which citizens can participate directly in the decision-making process, and are often resorted to by governments to allow direct input from the civilian population on questions of grave public importance. For example, referendums are often used to determine the popular will on questions of self-determination. Because referendums allow civilians a direct voice on issues of public importance, they can provide an opportunity to accurately gauge the will of the people.

Like all peoples, Ugandans have the right to freely choose their system of governance. However, two major issues seriously call into question whether the proposed referendum can truly be called a free and fair exercise of their democratic rights.

First, the NRM has extensively manipulated the political landscape in Uganda for the past thirteen years, and has succeeded to a significant extent in destroying the capacity of opposition political parties to function effectively. The demonization of independent political parties has been a central tenet of the NRM's political program, bolstered by a state-funded political education program which has immersed thousands into the ruling NRM's anti-party political ideology. While independent political parties have been systematically harassed, the NRM bodies (including the movement structures) have gained increased access to state funding and other state resources. Even during the pre-referendum campaign period, the political playing field between the opposition parties and the NRM will be fundamentally uneven. The track record of the NRM towards independent political parties suggests that harassment during the campaign period will be severe, effective preventing the advocates of pluralism from contesting the NRM's position. In short, the NRM will be in a position of unchallenged dominance during the referendum campaign period.

Second, the notion that fundamental human rights of freedom of association and assembly can be limited by a popular mandate is irreconcilable with the very purpose of human rights law, which is to put certain basic rights beyond the grasp of majority opinion. As the Ugandan constitution states, "fundamental rights and freedoms of the individual are inherent and not granted by the State."[256] The current limitations which the "movement" system of government places on the rights of freedom of association, assembly, speech and expression are inconsistent with Uganda's own constitution and with international law, and the referendum

---

[256]Uganda Constitution (1995), article 20(1).

aims to entrench these limitations further.[257] Ugandans are free to choose their political system by majority mandate, but the political system chosen must be consistent with the international human rights obligations assumed by the Ugandan government.

Regardless of the popular mandate which the NRM government may have in Uganda, fundamental human rights cannot be limited by a majority mandate. As argued by Mahmood Mamdani, professor for African Studies at the University of Cape Town,

> The consequence of a movement election is to make organized opposition illegal. That this can be decided by majority vote makes a travesty of the right of organized opposition, crucial to any democracy, since everyone knows that an opposition is just that, precisely because it is a minority.[258]

This was a view echoed by Norbert Mao, a member of parliament for Gulu municipality:

> I don't think political rights should be subject to a referendum. I am opposed to subjecting my freedom to associate to a referendum. The purpose of a bill of rights is to put certain rights beyond the reach of majorities. These are fundamental human rights which you enjoy not

---

[257]The comments of U.S. Supreme Court Justice Jackson, discussing the U.S. Bill of Rights, are equally apt in the context of the human rights protected by the international bill of rights:

> The very purpose of a bill of rights was to withdraw certain subjects from the vicissitudes of political controversy, to place them beyond the reach of majorities and officials and to establish them as legal principles to be applied by the courts. One's right to life, liberty, and property, to free speech, a free press, freedom of worship and assembly and other fundamental human rights may not be submitted to vote; they depend on the outcome of no election.

West Virginia Board of Education v. Barnette, 319 U.S. 625 (1943), p. 638.
    [258]Mahmood Mamdani, "What was that trip all about?," *The Monitor*, April 10, 1998, p. 31.

because you are many but because you are human. They are now turning it into a game of numbers.[259]

---

[259]Human Rights Watch interview with Norbert Mao MP (Gulu Municipality), Kampala, April 8, 1998.

VI. CIVIL SOCIETY AND THE MEDIA IN UGANDA

One of the most notable improvements in Uganda has been in the relative freedom given to the NGO community and the press. Uganda is home to a number of independent newspapers, some of which are frequently critical of the government. The Human Rights Network of Uganda (HURINET), a consortium of human rights NGOs in Uganda, currently has twenty-five member organizations. The Human Rights and Peace Centre (HURIPEC) at Makerere University has been able to make human rights education a central part of the education of all university students and is considered to be one of the preeminent academic human rights institutions in Africa.[260] Human Rights Watch attended a seminar sponsored by the Centre for Basic Research in Kampala in May 1998 where academics and politicians debated the movement system in a frank and open manner, seemingly without fear of retaliation. Despite this apparent openness, however, there are limits placed on the work of human rights NGOs and the media in Uganda.

Restrictions on NGO Activities

Ugandan human rights NGOs operate throughout the country, although the vast majority are based in the capital Kampala and conduct only limited activities outside the capital. Human rights groups such as the Foundation for Human Rights Initiative (FHRI) in Kampala and Human Rights Focus (HURIFO) in Gulu carry out some limited human rights investigative work, while the Uganda Law Society (ULS) and the Uganda Association of Women Lawyers (FIDA-U) represent some victims of human rights violations in court. The vast majority of human rights work carried out in Uganda is human rights education.

Several groups interviewed by Human Rights Watch claimed that they felt compelled to practice a significant amount of self-censorship to avoid confrontations with the government. This includes the issues they monitor: they normally focus on such issues such as prison reform, but rarely touch more controversial issues such as army abuses and the political restrictions associated with the movement system. However, a growing number of NGOs in Uganda are becoming increasingly willing to address army abuses and other "sensitive" areas of human rights abuses, partly encouraged by the work of the official Ugandan Human Rights Commission in these areas. But human rights NGOs continue to feel that the government is hostile to their work. A leading human rights activist

---

[260]Andrea Useem, "A Human Rights Center in Uganda Combines Academics With Activism," *Chronicle of Higher Education*, July 3, 1998, p. A33.

in Uganda described the attitude of the government towards human rights groups as follows:

> Museveni has said that human rights organizations are just blowing hot air and squandering money. Within this region, from Rwanda to Eritrea, you see a new brand of leaders. They are supposed to be enlightened despots. They accept the need for human rights to exist for their image, but do not believe in their inherent worth. In Uganda, we are tolerated as long as we censor ourselves. If we touch some buttons, we would be in trouble.[261]

The Ugandan government exercises significant control over NGO activities through the Non-Governmental Organizations Registration Statute, which requires that all NGOs operating in Uganda be registered. According to some NGO representatives, this process of registration is sometimes manipulated by the government in order to silence its critics. The National Board for Non-Governmental Organizations, created under this statute, includes representatives of a number of security organizations (the internal security organization (ISO) and the external security organization (ESO)). It has the power to revoke registration if it deems this to be in the "public interest."[262]

The control exercised by the National Board over the registration of NGOs presents a significant curb on the allowed activities of NGOs. According to Sheila Kawamara, coordinator of the Uganda Women's Network (UWONET), "They often remind us of our registration, which requires us to be nonpolitical, nonpartisan, noneverything. So whenever there is controversy, they tell us we are violating our statute."[263] NGOs are required to renew their registration after the first year, and thereafter every three years. By delaying their response to registration renewal requests, the NGO Board can exert significant pressure over NGOs. UWONET is one group which had received no response to its registration renewal request at the time of Human Rights Watch's visit.

Refusal to Register Uganda National NGO Forum
Several NGOs have apparently overstepped the boundaries established by the government and have been subjected to government harassment. One of the long-

---

[261]Human Rights Watch interview, Kampala, April 7, 1998.

[262]Non-Governmental Organizations Registration Statute (1989), Article 9.

[263]Human Rights Watch interview with Sheila Kawamara, coordinator, Uganda Women's Network, Kampala, April 6, 1998.

running cases of government interference with the activities of a civil society group has been the refusal of the government to register the Uganda National NGO Forum ("the NGO Forum"). The NGO Forum has stated that its aim is to provide a common forum for all domestic, foreign, and international NGOs active in Uganda, in order to enhance dialogue between the NGO community and the government, and to promote networking and information exchange between NGOs. Sheila Kawarama, the coordinator of the UWONET, is also one of the driving forces behind the NGO Forum and explained its purpose, as well as the hostility with which the government has reacted to its formation:

> We have been trying to get our national NGO Forum registered since 1995. But the government tries to divide us, they say that foreign NGOs should not discuss internal affairs because they are serving foreign governments. In issues of policy dialogue and human rights, we want to talk with a common voice. We bring out our issues and address them collectively. But the government wants us to talk individually, which weakens our voice. [As a women's group] we do not just wish to talk about women's rights, because many other issues affect our lives. ... We have a right as civil society to form our own organizations.[264]

The NGO Network filed all the necessary paperwork for registration in November 1997, and paid its mandatory 15,000 shilling registration fee at the same time. After repeated requests by the NGO Forum for action on the registration application, the NGO Board replied in March 1998 that the application had been "deferred until further notice" because the government was in the process of amending its legislation governing NGOs. The letter also stated that the "issue of you being a spokesperson and representative for all Foreign, International and Community Based Organisations was also revisited," suggesting that the NGO Board was uncomfortable with the idea of such a broad coalition. The NGO Board further said it wanted to research the functioning of similar broad coalitions in neighboring countries. The letter suggested that the government saw the NGO Forum as a possible competitor for its own, government-organized but nonfunctioning NGO Council:

> As you might be aware, there is a decision by cabinet pending the legal formation of the National Council of Voluntary Social Services (NCVSS). The cabinet approved the bill in 1992 to establish this body,

---

[264]Ibid.

whose role in governing NGOs might be the same roles as you would
like to play.

The letter ended with a strong warning to the NGO Forum to suspend its activities:
"You are meanwhile advised not to coordinate activities of NGOs directly, handle
policy dialogue with NGOs individually, lobby government or donors directly until
your registration is formalized."[265]
    The attitude of the government towards the NGO Forum is not always
consistent. In October 1998, the NGO Board replied again to enquiries from the
NGO Forum, stating that "the status quo remains the same" on the registration of
the NGO Forum, and refusing to arrange a meeting between the NGO Forum and
the NGO Board to discuss the registration application of the former. At the same
time, while explicitly affirming that the March 1998 warning to suspend its
activities (including government lobbying) still stood, the October letter asked the
NGO Forum to give the NGO Board input on its proposals for the restructuring of
the NGO Board.[266] Similarly, in November 1998, the office of the prime minister
invited the NGO Forum to participate in a workshop on national NGO policy and
asked the NGO Forum to make a twenty-minute presentation stating the position
of the network on the national NGO policy, even though the NGO Board had still
not registered the NGO Forum.[267]
    The issue of the registration of the NGO Forum again gained prominence
when it attempted to organize a consultative meeting on the proposed national
policy for NGOs in March 1999. The NGO Forum invited the office of the prime
minister to attend the opening of the meeting and to send a representative to attend
the entire proceedings. The office of the prime minister replied with a threatening
letter, again stating that the NGO Forum could not engage in any activities until it
had obtained registration, concluding:

   [I]t would be improper for any Government official to attend this kind
   of meeting in an Official Capacity. By copy of this letter, I am
   requesting my colleague in the Ministry of Internal Affairs to stop you
   from doing the right thing in the wrong way.

[265]Letter of Joni Kasigaire, secretary of the NGO Board, to the coordinator of National
NGO Forum, dated March 19, 1998.
[266]Letter of Joni Kasigaire, secretary of the NGO Board, to the coordinator of Uganda
National NGO Forum, dated October 1, 1998.
[267]Letter from Peter Ucanda, permanent secretary, office of the prime minister, to
executive secretary of the NGO Forum, November 16, 1998.

In the meanwhile, you are advised that the proposed NGO "FORUM" cannot conduct policy dialogue with government, lobby government and be a spokesman for the registered NGOs and the civil society in the country until registered as a NGO as well.[268]

The NGO Forum proceeded with its planned consultative meeting, and informed the prime minister's office of the resolutions taken at the meeting.[269]

On May 27, 1999, the NGO Forum organized its second general assembly at the International Conference Center in Kampala. According to the organizers, the general assembly meeting was well publicized and the meeting was attended by representatives of more than 260 national, foreign and international NGOs. At about 11 a.m., two plainclothes policemen who identified themselves as belonging to Kampala Central Police Station entered the meeting hall, approached the organizers and ordered them to stop the "illegal meeting." The organizers demanded to see a letter authorizing the break-up of the meeting, and the police officers returned shortly afterwards with a letter from Inspector General of the Police J. Kisembo entitled "Illegal Acts by Uganda NGO Forum," which referred to the fact that the NGO Forum was "not duly registered as a required by the law" and ordered the organizers to "immediately stop the said meeting which has been unlawfully constituted."[270] The delegates at the NGO Forum decided to end the meeting peacefully and avoid a confrontation with the police.[271]

Revocation of UHEDOC Registration

The Uganda Human Rights and Documentation Centre (UHEDOC) has experienced similar registration problems. In November 1996, UHEDOC held a well-attended seminar on corruption in Uganda, featuring Winnie Byanyima, an outspoken member of parliament, as the keynote speaker. When UHEDOC tried to renew its registration a few days after the seminar, it was stonewalled. For the next months, UHEDOC regularly sent its representatives to the registration office at the Ministry of Internal Affairs to check on the registration process. When a British consultant at UHEDOC was denied access to Luzira prison on the grounds

---

[268]Letter of F. B. Nshemeire, permanent secretary, office of the prime minister, to the coordinator of the NGO Forum, dated April 27, 1999.

[269]Letter of Rauxen Zedriga, coordinator, NGO Forum, to the permanent secretary of the office of the prime minister, dated May 17, 1999.

[270]Letter of J. Kisembo, inspector general of police, to chairperson of the National NGO Forum, dated May 27, 1999.

[271]Email of Rauxen Zedriga to Human Rights Watch, dated June 2, 1999.

that the organization was not registered, she approached the minister of internal affairs, Major Tom Butime. According to a UHEDOC source, the minister phoned the UHEDOC offices after the meeting:

> He was very furious, asking why we had sent a muzungu [white] lady to his office and what we were doing as activities. He then asked whether our interests were to serve London or Copenhagen [the source of some UHEDOC funding], and before banging down the phone, he said we were no more as an organization. This was at 11 a.m. At 1:30 p.m., we received a notice that we were terminated as an organization in the public interest. We thought that this could only be done through the NGO board, which allows for an appeal to the minister. Since the minister himself issued the order, whom could we appeal to? What followed then was a long process of underground negotiations. ... We had not known that NGOs practice this self-censorship. Anybody who does opposition activities or is seen as doing this is frustrated by paper, not physically threatened.[272]

Before agreeing to restore UHEDOC's certificate of registration, the minister of internal affairs made it clear that they must function without political overtones: "So we are now operating on the basis of being good people, not anti-government, and within the parameters of the unwritten rules which can be perceived by those who are not blind."[273]

Delay in Registration of NOCEM

The National Organization for Civic Education and Elections Monitoring (NOCEM), which is an umbrella NGO consisting of twelve community-based NGOs,[274] had similar problems with the registration process. NOCEM was formed in 1993, prior to the constituent assembly elections, in order to provide independent civic education and elections monitoring. According to the NOCEM chairperson,

---

[272]Human Rights Watch interview with UHEDOC source, Kampala, April 9, 1998.
[273]Ibid.
[274]The member organizations of NOCEM are: the Uganda Law Society, the Uganda Prisoners Aid Foundation, FIDA-Uganda, Action for Development, Uganda Journalists Association, Foundation for Human Rights Initiative, Uganda Human Rights Activists, Youth Alliance for Development and Cooperation, Islamic Information Centre, Federation for Professional and Business Women, Sustain Africa, and Uganda Community Based Child Association.

Mr. Zirabamuzaale, the registration of NOCEM took almost three years because the government was concerned about the participation of multipartyists in NOCEM and about the rapid growth of NOCEM monitoring branches throughout the country:

> Our structures grew very fast and this worried the government. There were multipartyists involved in NOCEM, but also NRM supporters. The government studied our structures carefully, and a member of the NGO Board told us that the Internal Security Organization (ISO) had requested our files. The registration took us about three years. They just would not respond to our requests for information. They told us that there was a backlog, but meanwhile they were registering others who had applied later. They kept telling us that unless we sweep house, we would not get registered. I think they meant that we should get rid of multipartyists, but this was impossible since we have no control over the membership of our member organizations. We were finally registered on December 4, 1995.[275]

A number of recent incidents of government interference with civil society in Uganda are documented in this report's discussion of the right to freedom of assembly. These incidents include the last minute cancellation of a Kampala peace march sponsored by the church and NGO in March, 1998, on the apparent grounds that the march could be turned into a political event, and the breaking up of a series of seminars on the topic of "Human Rights and Democracy" sponsored by the Foundation for African Development (FAD) and the Uganda Young Democrats (UYD). A single theme running through most of these incidents is that they all took place in response to perceived attempts by groups to discuss or document "political" topics. Thus, civil society in Uganda continues to be effectively prevented from addressing some of the most pressing human rights issues in Uganda, namely the political restrictions which operate under the movement system.

NRM Efforts to Organize Civil Society

The NRM-led government has organized a number of NRM-controlled and aligned organs that extend into broad sectors of civil society. In 1993, the government established the National Association of Women's Organizations in

---

[275]Human Rights Watch interview with J.K. Zirabamuzaale, chairperson, NOCEM, Kampala, April 15, 1998.

Uganda (NAWOU), which is facilitated by the Ministry of Women in Development. As discussed above, the NRM government has also attempted to form an all-encompassing NGO forum, the National Council of Voluntary Social Services. The NRM has been especially active in the area of youth mobilization: in 1988, the NRM convened a meeting which led to the establishment of the Uganda National Students Association (UNSA) and in 1994 Youth Councils were established by the government at all local council levels: "The Councils, which are financed by the government, are integrated into the government accounting system and are to be audited by the auditor general. The Secretary General of the National Youth Council is appointed by the Minister in charge of youth."[276]

Furthermore, attempts by NGOs to organize themselves into broader coalitions have been resisted by the Ugandan government, which originally refused to register the independent Uganda Women's Network (UWONET). According to Sheila Kawamara, its coordinator:

> The government wants to form its own NGO forums. They do not want NGOs to come together and speak with one voice. When UWONET was first formed, the government refused to register us. The government told us, "Why do you claim to speak on behalf of women when there is a women's ministry?" The government is skeptical of NGOs, they think we will turn into political parties. We have been trying to get our national NGO forum registered since 1995.... But the government wants us to talk individually, which weakens our voice.[277]

President Museveni has often been critical of the work of human rights groups in Uganda, urging them to focus on abuses by rebel groups instead of government abuses. A large consortium of human rights NGOs asked Museveni to consider peace talks with rebel groups and raised concerns about a spate of arbitrary arrests and allegations of torture by security forces with Museveni in June 1998. Museveni responded by rejecting compromise and urging the human rights organizations to focus on rebel abuses instead of government practices: "You human rights groups should instead demand that these criminals are arrested.... Actually there should be more arrests because you cannot imagine the number of people who have been killed by extra-judicial means by these criminals. Do they

---

[276]Akiiki B. Mujaju, "Civil Society at Bay in Uganda," p. 48.
[277]Human Rights Watch interview with Sheila Kawamara, coordinator, Uganda Women's Network, Kampala, April 6, 1998.

respect human rights? Why don't you ask them?"[278] Abuses committed by rebel groups, however grave, do not justify human rights abuses by government forces. Museveni again responded with hostility when journalist raised allegations of UPDF abuses against rebel suspects in July 1998:

> We are going to be very ruthless with these people. I should ask you journalists to show more indignation towards those criminals than towards the government...You do not care about the human rights of innocent victims of terrorism. [The rebels] will get what they are giving to our people. We are now roasting them in the mountains [Rwenzori], these cowards... We have been too soft. I do not want to hear of those fellows.[279]

Restrictions on Press Freedom

Uganda has a vocal and independent press in addition to the government-owned *New Vision* newspaper. Some opposition political parties publish newspapers, such as the UPC's *People* newspaper. There are more than twenty independent newspapers and magazines which often express opinions highly critical of government policies and practices, including the movement system of government. Minister of Information Dr. Ruhakana Ruganda has occasionally spoken favorably of press freedom, arguing that it not only benefits journalists but also society: "It is like a doctor feeling the patient's pulse, you see what the problem is and work on it."[280] After a conference at which press freedom in Uganda was praised, the East Africa Media Institute decided to shift its secretariat from Nairobi to Kampala, citing "bureaucratic bottlenecks" in Kenya.[281]

Despite these positive developments, the Ugandan government continues to detain and charge journalists under repressive sedition and "publishing false news" legislation, causing journalists to practice self-censorship. The paradoxical contrast in Uganda between a vocal and diverse press and the regular arrests and prosecutions of leading media figures results in part from the draconian press laws which remain on the books, despite the constitutionally guaranteed right to freedom of the press. Some of the laws used to prosecute journalists, such as the law on seditious libel, date back to the colonial era. The sedition statutes give the

---

[278]Alfred Wasike, "Museveni Rejects Rebel Compromise," *New Vision*, June 20, 1998.

[279]"No Ceasefire, Says Museveni," *New Vision*, July 22, 1998.

[280]Nabusayi L. Wamboka, "Free Press Good For Society—Rugunda," *Monitor*, May 4, 1998, p. 28.

[281]"Institute Shifts to Kampala," *New Vision*, May 7, 1998.

government draconian powers to arrest and prosecute journalists who raise the government's ire, as demonstrated in the cases outlined below. In 1995, the Press and Journalists Law came in effect after its adoption by the non-elected National Resistance Council. The law requires all journalists to be licenced, and provides for a media council which monitors and disciplines journalists and editors. While the media council is empowered to arbitrate disputes between the media and the State, to discipline journalists, and "to regulate the conduct and promote good ethical standards and discipline of journalists," the government rarely resorts to the Council for the resolution of disputes with the media, preferring to rely on more severe criminal sanctions instead.[282]

The Press and Journalists Law of 1995 and the various criminal statutes such as sedition and criminal libel which are used against journalists are vigorously opposed by journalists as a limit on the freedom of the press. In June 1997, the Uganda Journalists Safety Committee brought two petitions in the constitutional court, one challenging the press and journalists law and another challenging the sedition and criminal libel sections of the criminal code. The petitions were dismissed in December 1997.

Prominent incidents of detention, arrest, and prosecution of journalists include:

* On December 20, 1998, James Mujuni, the Mbarara correspondent for the government-owned *New Vision* newspaper, was reportedly arrested at the newspaper's Mbarara office by three plainclothes members of the district's criminal investigations department (CID). He was later charged with "promoting sectarianism." The charges appear to be related to articles he wrote on November 9 and 12 about the proliferation of guns among Bahima herdsmen in the Mbarara cattle corridor, Museveni's home region. The *New Vision* newspaper reported that District Police Commissioner Walter Ogom stated that the arrest "had been directed from Kampala."[283] Mujuni was transferred to Kampala, where he was questioned for several hours and kept overnight before being released. Mujuni later said that the police asked him to serve as a witness against George Lugalambi, editor of the *Crusader* newspaper, who had been arrested on December 17, 1998, and charged with "promoting sectarianism" (see below).[284]

---

[282]Press and Journalist Statute (no. 6 of 1995), section 10.

[283]"Journalist Arrested, Charged with 'Promoting Sectarianism,'" *New Vision*, December 20, 1998.

[284]"Vision Scribe Grilled," *New Vision*, December 21, 1998.

- On December 17, 1998 four armed policemen, including one with an AK-47 assault rifle, raided the offices of the *Crusader* newspaper in Kampala, confiscating some documents which they reportedly described as "seditious material." The editor of the *Crusader*, George Lugalambi, and a staff reporter, Meddie Musini, were taken away by the policemen and kept overnight at the police station for questioning. The next day, Lugalambi was charged with promoting sectarianism for publishing an article on entitled "Karuhanga's Excuse for Arming Bahima is Nonsense," relating to the arming of Bahima herdsmen in the Mbarara cattle corridor. Lugalambi was released on cash bail of 300,000 Uganda shillings (about U.S. $300) and three sureties of 5 million shillings (about U.S. $5,000) each.[285]

  The Committee to Protect Journalists (CPJ) wrote to President Museveni to express its concerns about the case, stating that it believed that the arrest and prosecution of Lugalambi "is a warning from the government to Uganda's journalists, that those who report on issues such as official corruption, ethnic tension, and human rights will face reprisals from the government."[286]

  Following the arrest, Amos Kajuba, President of the East African Media Institute, met with Ugandan Minister of Information Basoga Nsanju on December 19, 1998, to express his concerns about a recent spate of arrests of journalists over the publication of political statements, and urged that complaints be handled by the government-established Media Council rather than through criminal charges. The minister reportedly replied by urging editors to practice self-censorship before publishing sensitive stories.[287]

- On October 29, 1998, Kevin Ogen Aliro, an editor at the *Monitor* newspaper, sustained serious injuries, including a compound collarbone fracture and a fractured shoulder blade, after being attacked by six unidentified assailants. Aliro could not recognize his assailants, but they knew him by name and profession. One called him by his first name. Another shouted at him "this

---

[285]"Police raid newspaper offices, arrest editor," *New Vision*, December 18, 1998; "Newspaper Editor, Opposition Leader Charged, Released on Bail," *New Vision*, December 19, 1998.

[286]Letter of Ann K. Cooper, Executive Director, Committee to Protect Journalists, to President Yoweri Museveni, dated December 18, 1998.

[287]"East African Media Official Expresses Concern About Journalists," *Radio Uganda*, December 19, 1998 (reported on BBC Monitoring).

will teach you to keep your big mouth shut." Aliro believes that the attack was in retaliation for an article entitled "Safe Houses: A Return to the Shadows," published in the *Monitor* on October 27, 1998. The article presented strong evidence that the internal security organization (ISO) and other intelligence agencies were torturing terrorism suspects in secret "safe houses" around Kampala.[288]

• On June 2, 1998, Mulindwa Muwonge, host of the *Ekijja Omanya* program on the independent Central Broadcasting Station (CBS), was detained and interrogated by the police in Kampala.[289] The questioning focused around the "dangerous" remarks made by Muwonge on a May 31, 1998 broadcast about the proposed Land Bill, legislation widely disliked by Buganda leaders. The radio station was publicly criticized by Museveni who blamed the station for "inciting the public to rise against the constitution."[290]

Earlier, the minister of information, Ruhakana Rugunda, threatened to refer CBS to the Media Council because "it has been inciting people instead of explaining the [land] bill to them."[291] The minister of state for local government compared Muwonge's work to that of the extremist Radio Milles Collines in Rwanda:

This is very dangerous. There is this man called Muwonge Mulindwa with his program on CBS. We request you to slow down. You remember what happened in Rwanda. ... You can see the extent to which irresponsible journalism can go. It can plunge our country into genocide.[292]

The CBS incident coincided with other attempts by the government to limit the public debate on the proposed land bill, such as the arrest of outspoken

---

[288]Human Rights Watch interview with Ogen Kevin Aliro, Chief Sub-Editor of *Monitor* newspaper, November 14, 1998.

[289]"CID Quizzes CBS' Muwonge for 4 Hours," *Monitor*, June 4, 1998; "CID Summons CBS' Muwonge," *Monitor*, June 3, 1998.

[290]"Museveni Blasts Mengo over land," *New Vision*, June 2, 1998.

[291]Peter Okello Jabweli, "Government Cautions CBS Radio," *New Vision*, May 20, 1998.

[292]Alfred Wasike, "Land—Otafiire fears genocide," *New Vision*, May 11, 1998; "Minister warns private radios against inciting Rwanda-style violence," *Radio Uganda*, May 10, 1998, 17:00gmt.

members of parliament opposed to the land bill and police interference with public events opposing the land bill discussed above in this report.

- Loy Nabeta, assistant editor of the *Monitor*, and *Monitor* senior writer Pius Katunzi were questioned for several hours in Kampala on April 22, 1998. The two had published an "April Fools" day story in the *Monitor* under the title "Pulkol Flees to Sudan: Senior UPDF Officers arrested." The story suggested that senior UPDF officers had been arrested after a plan to assassinate U.S. President Clinton had been uncovered, and that the director-general of external security (ESO), David Pulkol, had fled to Sudan after his role in the plot had been uncovered. The story carried a clear disclaimer at the end, stating: "However we do hope that you enjoy your Fool's Day and don't take this as a true story."[293]

- CBS presenter Mulindwa Muwonge was summoned for questioning in Kampala in March 1998 for making "irrational statements" on the radio. Police accused Muwonge of exposing a police informant on the radio.[294]

- On October 24, 1997, *Monitor* editor Charles Onyango Obbo and reporter Andrew Mwenda were arrested and charged with "publishing false news" after a story appeared in the *Monitor* on September 21, 1997, entitled "Kabila paid Uganda in Gold, says report." The story was based on a report by the Paris-based *Indian Ocean Newsletter*, claiming that President Kabila of the Democratic Republic of Congo paid Uganda in gold for Uganda's support of his anti-Mobutu rebellion. At a graduation ceremony soldiers in Jinja on the day after the story appeared President Museveni spoke in anger against the story and vowed to punish the paper and the journalists.

  The journalists were released on bail of 2 million Ugandan shillings (about U.S. $2,000) each and sureties of 5 million Ugandan shillings (about U.S. $5,000) each, a bail amount which was condemned as "unfair and unjustifiable" by the Uganda Journalists' Safety Committee, a media watchdog organization.[295] The bail amount was the highest ever imposed for a misdemeanor offense. The bail was later reduced to 200,000 Ugandan

---

[293]"Journalists in Big Trouble Over Fool's Day Story," *Monitor*, April 23, 1998.

[294]Joyce Namutebi, "Central Broadcasting Service Presenter Summoned for Questioning," *New Vision*, March 3, 1998.

[295]"Journalists protest over 'harsh bail' in Monitor case," *East African*, November 3, 1997.

shillings each (about U.S. $200) after a successful appeal to the high court.[296] Senior presidential adviser on media and public relations John Nagenda testified in the case that the publication of the story was a treasonable offense in his view.[297] The two journalists were acquitted in February 1999, when a magistrate held that although the allegations in the story were false, they had not caused fear or alarm to the public.[298]

• The Committee to Protect Journalists reported in July 1997 that Henry Tumwine, a reporter with *New Vision*, was arrested by soldiers at Fort Portal and taken to an undisclosed location. The arrest followed the publication of his article documenting the discovery of fifty-eight bodies in Bundibugyo, apparent victims of a massacre by Allied Democratic Forces (ADF) rebels.[299] The journalist was later released.

• Amos Kajoba, editor of the UPC-owned newspaper *People*, was detained for five hours on March 24, 1997, after publishing a report on a security meeting of West Nile community leaders, and had to report to police on at least five different occasions afterwards.[300]

• The editor of the Lira-based *Rupiny* newspaper was briefly detained in April 1997 by police for allegedly publishing negative reports about Lira municipality.[301]

• Editors of the *Monitor* were detained and questioned in February 1997 by police following the publication of news articles which apparently angered President Museveni.[302]

---

[296]"Obbo, Mwenda cash Shs 3.6m from Court," *Monitor*.

[297]Pauline Mbabazi, "Monitor Gold Story Was Treasonable—Nagenda," *New Vision*, April 28, 1998.

[298]"Monitor Editor Acquitted," *New Vision*, Feb. 17, 1999; "Ugandan journalists acquitted on false news charge," Agence France Presse, February 17, 1999.

[299]Committee to Protect Journalists, "Henry Tumwine," Press Freedom Database (1997).

[300]"Index-Index," *Index on Censorship*, May/June 1997.

[301]U.S. Department of State, Bureau of Democracy, Human Rights, and Labor, *Uganda Country Report on Human Rights Practices for 1997* (January 30, 1998).

[302]Ibid.

- On December 4, 1996, Peter Busiku, editor of the weekly *Uganda Express,* was arrested by plainclothes policemen and charged with publishing "false statements or reports which are likely to cause fear and alarm to the public." The arrest followed the publication of an article entitled "Uganda, Burundi, Rwanda plan assault on Tanzania," alleging that Uganda was involved with Rwanda and Burundi in planning attacks on Hutu refugees in Zairian and Tanzanian refugee camps.[303] His trial began on May 21, 1997, before Magistrate Precious Nyabriano in Kampala. Rwandan Vice-President Paul Kagame admitted in a July 1997 interview that Rwanda had planned attacks on the Zairian refugee camps, and Uganda has also been shown to have been deeply involved in Kabila's ADFL rebel campaign which carried out the attacks.[304]

- On October 3, 1996, Mulindwa Muwonge, the CBS radio journalist, was arrested, interrogated, and detained overnight. CBS had broadcast interviews of people discussing the stand-off between government and traders who were striking to protest a recently introduced VAT tax. The minister of internal affairs had issued a statement on October 1, 1996, warning that anyone who encouraged the strike would be arrested.

- Teddy Sseezi-Cheeye, editor of *Uganda Confidential* and a critic of the Museveni government, has been subjected to court proceedings on a number of occasions. He was arrested on January 21, 1996 and kept in solitary confinement. His wife claimed that she was denied the opportunity to visit her husband while he was in detention. He was released four days later.

  In a separate case, Cheeye was found innocent in January 1997 of having kidnapped a woman for sexual purposes, with the chief magistrate commenting that the charges were "a frame-up engineered by powerful and corrupt people" whom Cheeye had previously criticized for corruption.[305]

---

[303]Committee to Protect Journalists, "Journalist Peter Busiku charged with publishing 'false news,'" December 6, 1996.

[304]Africa Division of Human Rights Watch, "What Kabila is Hiding: Civilian Killings and Impunity in the Congo," *A Human Rights Watch Short Report* vol. 9, no. 5(A) (New York: Human Rights Watch, October 1997); John Pomfret, "Rwanda Planned and Led the Attack on Zaire," *Washington Post*, July 9, 1997.

[305]U.S. Department of State, Bureau of Democracy, Human Rights, and Labor, *Uganda Country Report on Human Rights Practices for 1997* (January 30, 1998).

Cheeye was convicted in 1996 of defaming Chief Justice Wambuzi, and continues to face various libel cases brought by individuals who have been the targets of his highly personalized editorials.

Cheeye was previously arrested and charged with sedition in 1993, after running a series of articles accusing the president's wife of involvement in her cousin's murder over a land dispute, and accusing the Uganda Revenue Authority of "politically inspired nepotism."

• On August 25, 1995, Hussein Musa Njuki, editor of the Islamic opposition weekly *Assalaam*, and Haruna Kanaabi, editor of the Islamic opposition weekly *Shariat*, were arrested by members of the anti-robbery squad, a division of the ISO. Njuki was to be charged with sedition for publishing an article entitled "Multiparty democracy will not return to Uganda until Museveni dies." Kanaabi was arrested for publishing a tongue-in-cheek article entitled "Rwanda is now a Ugandan province."

Forty-two-year-old Njuki died in police custody three days after his arrest, most likely because of deteriorating health which may have been exacerbated by his incarceration.

Kanaabi was denied bail on the grounds that the editor of a different paper, Lawrence Kiwanuka of the *Citizen*, had recently fled the country while on bail (see below). Kanaabi was convicted of sedition and publishing false news in December 1995, and sentenced to five months imprisonment: he was released soon after sentencing for time served while awaiting trial. The conviction was affirmed by the high court on November 13, 1996. Kanaabi and Njuki had previously been detained and charged with sedition in October 1993 in conjunction with the publication in *Shariat* of a letter to the editor which expressed the opinion that "Museveni and his gang of thieves are destroying the country."

• On April 13, 1995, Lawrence Kiwanuka, editor of the DP paper *Citizen*, was arrested and held incommunicado at Kampala central police station for a week, until April 20, 1995, when he was released on bail of one million shillings (about U.S. $580) and two sureties valued at U.S. $17,000 each.[306] He was charged with two counts of "publishing false information likely to cause disaffection within the state." The charges related to the publication of an article quoting a letter by members of the External Security Organization

---

[306]"Detained Ugandan editor charged, but released on bail," Agence France Presse, April 20, 1995.

(ESO) accusing the government of support for Sudanese and Kenyan rebel groups.[307] Kiwanuka also accused the Ugandan army of fighting alongside the Rwanda Patriotic Front (RPF) in Rwanda, and had conducted interviews with leaders of the newly-formed National Democratic Alliance (NDA) rebel movement.[308] *New Vision* claimed that security officials wanted Kiwanuka to lead them to the NDA rebel camps where he had conducted interviews and which he had photographed.[309]

Kiwanuka fled to Kenya on May 10, claiming that he had been tipped off that his life was in danger. Two journalists who stood surety for Kiwanuka, Nasser Ssebagala and the editor of the monthly *Exposure* Henry Mirima, were jailed for a week after Kiwanuka fled. According to the Committee to Protect Journalists, Kiwanuka and his family were granted asylum by the United States in August 1995 after an apparent attempt by Ugandan ESO agents to abduct him in Kenya.[310]

---

[307]Edward Kizito, "Uganda arrests journalist on sedition charge," Reuters World Service, April 14, 1995.

[308]"Police Arrest Editor of Ugandan Weekly," Agence France Presse, April 14, 1995. The NDA was a short-lived rebel group formed in the Buganda area in 1995 following the rejection of federalist and multipartyist proposals in the constituent assembly.

[309]"Ugandan government fails to produce detained editor in court," Agence France Presse, April 18, 1995.

[310]Committee to Protect Journalists, "Lawrence Kiwanuka," Press Freedom Database (1995).

VII. THE MOVEMENT SYSTEM AND THE CONFLICTS IN
WESTERN AND NORTHERN UGANDA

The peace, prosperity, and stability around Kampala leaves one little prepared for the almost complete destruction which rebel conflicts in the west and north of Uganda have left in their wake. In the north, where a rebellion has been active for more than fourteen years under various banners, currently under that of the Lord's Resistance Army led by Joseph Kony, the entire infrastructure lies in shambles and the majority of the population are forced to live under dire conditions in "protected villages." An earlier Human Rights Watch report described the gulf between north and south:

> It is only a four-hour drive from Kampala to Gulu or Kitgum, but it might as well be a thousand miles. Cultural and linguistic differences ensure that residents of southern Uganda have few social reasons to venture north, and the relative under-development of the far north makes it unlikely that southerners will visit Gulu or Kitgum for commercial reasons. The danger of mines and ambushes along northern roads further diminishes southerners' incentive to visit their Acholi compatriots, and the lack of telecommunications infrastructure in the north makes even phone contact rare.[311]

Although more recent, the Allied Democratic Forces (ADF) conflict in Western Uganda is also creating a human rights and humanitarian crisis. Several other rebel movements also continue to operate in Uganda at lower levels of activity, such as the Uganda National Rescue Front II (UNRF II); the West Nile Bank Front (WNBF) made up predominately of Amin-era soldiers[312]; and the Uganda Peoples Army (UPA) headed by Peter Otai, minister of defense in Obote's second

---

[311]Children's Division of Human Rights Watch, *The Scars of Death: Children Abducted by the Lord's Resistance Army* (New York: Human Rights Watch, 1997), p. 60.
[312]A former LRA abductee told Human Rights Watch that remnants of the WNBF joined the LRA at the latter's Aru camp shortly after the WNBF's Morobo base was destroyed by the Sudanese Peoples' Liberation Army (SPLA, a predominantly Dinka-based Sudanese rebel group under the leadership of John Garang); the Aru camp was in turn attacked by a combined Ugandan army (UPDF) and SPLA force on April 9-10, 1998. Human Rights Watch interview with former LRA abductee, Gulu, May 2, 1998.

government.[313] In late 1998, a new rebel group calling itself the Uganda Salvation Army (USA) made an appearance in eastern Uganda, attacking Tororo prison and abducting a number of inmates. There have been repeated reports of collaboration and coordination between some of these rebel groups through meetings in Sudan.[314]

On May 31, 1999, six armed persons, most of them dressed in military uniforms, attacked the Boroboro police post on the outskirts of Lira. One policeman was killed in the attack, and another two were wounded. The rebels left behind a letter identifying themselves as the Citizens Army for Multiparty Politics (CAMP), and stating that they were fighting for the restoration of multiparty politics in Uganda.[315] According to the UPDF, the new rebel group was organized by the former chief of staff in Milton Obote's UNLA army, Brigadier Smith Opon Acak. Brigadier Acak was killed by UPDF soldiers during a July 18, 1999, ambush on a CAMP rebel training camp near Lira.[316]

Human Rights Abuses in Areas of Rebel Conflict

The Lord's Resistance Army (LRA) has been responsible for a campaign of terror against civilians in Northern Uganda. Supposedly dedicated to overthrowing the Museveni government, the LRA spends most of its time brutalizing and killing civilians, stealing their children, and looting and burning their homes. The LRA is mostly an army of abducted children, many as young as twelve. It is estimated that as many as 6,000 to 10,000 children have been abducted by the LRA for induction into their army. At times, the LRA has targeted schools and churches to abduct children en masse: such incidents took place in October 1996 at St. Mary's School in Aboke, Lira district, where the LRA abducted 139 girls, and in June 1998 at St. Charles Lwanga School in Kalongo, Kitgum district, where thirty-nine girls were abducted. Abducted children face a harsh and often deadly march to Sudan,

---

[313]Although some of these other rebel groups are relatively inactive at present, they continue to engage in periodic abuses. In June, *New Vision* reported that the UNRF II had abducted an estimated one hundred persons in a mass raid in Aringa county, Arua district. The paper also blamed UNRF II for several other attacks in the region including a raid on Palorinya health center where two health workers were abducted. Emmy Allio and Ahmed Angulibo, "Rebels Abduct 100 in Arua," *New Vision*, June 15, 1998.

[314]In July 1998, *New Vision* reported that a meeting of representatives of the LRA, ADF, UNRF-II, WNBF and an unknown rebel group calling itself the Former Uganda National Army (FUNA) took place in the Sudanese capital of Khartoum. "Ugandan rebel groups meet in Khartoum: Report," Agence France Presse, July 6, 1998.

[315]"'Rebels' invade Lira, kill cop," *Monitor*, June 3, 1999.

[316]"Slain Ex-Army Chief 'Planning Attack," United Nations IRIN-CEA, Update 719 for June 21, 1999.

and inhuman conditions in the Sudanese training camps. Those who attempt to escape are tortured and killed, most often by other recent abductees who are forced to participate in the killings. Abducted girls are "given" as "wives" to senior LRA commanders and face a life of sexual abuse and regular beatings. It is estimated that as many as 5,000 of the captive children have died during battle, from malnutrition or disease, or from LRA torture and execution; the children who manage to escape are scarred for life, forever reliving their brutal treatment and the atrocities they were forced to commit. The girls face the additional burden of often having been infected with sexually transmitted diseases, including HIV.

The LRA rarely engages in direct combat with the Ugandan army. Instead, it attacks civilians in direct violation of international humanitarian law protecting noncombatants. It sometimes seems that every civilian in the north can recount instances of LRA abuses. Villagers live in constant fear of LRA attacks. The LRA, normally operating in small units, move around the remote countryside, traveling from family compound to family compound and leaving a path of destruction in their wake. Civilians are routinely killed by the LRA for no apparent reason; belongings are looted. In order to enforce its rule of terror, the LRA has mutilated civilians: civilians seen riding or in possession of bicycles have had a foot cut off, local officials have had a hand amputated, and civilians have had their lips cut off to send a message to the government. The LRA has placed landmines throughout the northern districts of Uganda, and civilians are often injured and maimed by them. The testimonies of former abductees and the placement of the landmines on village footpaths suggest that the LRA deliberately targets civilians with them.

Much of the population of northern Uganda has been displaced by the LRA conflict. In November 1996, the Ugandan army, the Uganda People's Defense Force (UPDF), began placing the population into a series of "protected camps." The UPDF campaign to bring the civilian population to the protected camps was accompanied by significant violence and force, and civilians who refused to move were beaten or threatened with having their homes burned. The sites of the protected camps were not prepared with the necessary infrastructure to receive and accommodate the large number of displaced persons, and conditions in the camps continue to be harsh and inhuman. The population of the camps, denied the ability to cultivate food crops, is completely dependent on international humanitarian organizations for relief.

The presence of landmines and intermittent attacks by LRA rebels have always complicated the work of international humanitarian groups working with the internally displaced persons and Sudanese refugees in northern Uganda. In April 1998, the LRA issued a statement stating that they would consider these

NGOs "legitimate military targets" because the NGOs supported what the LRA called Museveni's "concentration camps." Food convoys of humanitarian groups such as the World Food Program (WFP) and Oxfam were attacked in the North, and heavy fighting in Kitgum district coupled with renewed LRA threats forced a temporary withdrawal from Kitgum district by most NGOs in May to June 1998. In December 1998, heightened insecurity in Gulu district again led to the interruption of humanitarian aid delivery when private transport companies canceled their delivery contracts out of fear of rebel attacks. Interference with the work of humanitarian organizations place large civilian populations that are completely dependent on humanitarian aid at great risk.

The UPDF has a difficult relationship with civilians in northern Uganda, based on historical animosities as well as a past record of UPDF abuses there. The UPDF's response to LRA attacks is often slow, and when the UPDF responds in time to engage the LRA in combat, civilians often get caught in the middle. Incidents of abuse and torture of suspected rebel sympathizers at UPDF barracks continues. One man was arbitrarily arrested and placed in an underground pit at Awer detachment in February 1998. He described having been tortured by having his testicles tied with a rope and being the victim of a mock live burial. In another case, soldiers beat the mother of a suspected rebel collaborator and burned down his compound when they did not find him at home. In a number of other cases, soldiers beat suspected collaborators. Eight civilians at Layik detachment in March 1998 were tied in the hazardous and outlawed *kandooya* method (involving the tying of the arms tightly together at the elbows behind the back) which can cause paralysis, and caned severely, while a woman who was arrested with them was raped at the same barracks. Human Rights Watch received many reports that soldiers, especially soldiers attached to the mobile units, commonly loot the abandoned compounds of displaced civilians. Several reports of rapes by soldiers were received by Human Rights Watch, and in some cases no action had been taken by the responsible authorities.

Since November 1996, the Allied Democratic Forces (ADF) has been engaged in a guerrilla war against the Ugandan government in the Rwenzori mountains in Western Uganda. The ADF is an alliance of at least three rebel groups, including the remnants of the secessionist Rwenzururu movement, the National Army for the Liberation of Uganda, and extremist elements from the Tabliq Muslim community. The activities of the ADF have become increasingly focused on civilians, who have faced the brunt of their violent abuses. It appears that the ADF is aiming to sow terror among the civilian population through attacks on civilians which often result in massacres. As one civilian victim of an ADF attack recounted to Human Rights Watch, "they just came to cut and kill." On occasion, the ADF has mutilated its victims, sometimes cutting off the ears of civilians or decapitating persons and, in at least one reported case, placing the head on a stake along a footpath. Several victims told Human Rights Watch that the ADF is brutalizing civilians because they are resentful at the lack of civilian support for their campaign against the Museveni government.

Like the LRA, the ADF has abducted a large number of children and adults for the purpose of forced recruitment into their rebel movement. The abductees are taken to remote training camps in the Rwenzori mountains or in the Democratic Republic of Congo where they receive rudimentary military training. Civilians are abducted from both Uganda and the Democratic Republic of Congo. Adults are also abducted, sometimes for the purpose of carrying looted goods back to the ADF camps. On several occasions, the ADF has conducted children en masse from schools. On August 16, 1997, the ADF attacked the St. John's Catholic Seminary in Kasese district, abducting nineteen seminarians and two workers. One worker was killed soon after the abduction by cutting his throat, and the abducted children were told that a similar fate awaited them if they attempted to escape. On February 19, 1998, the ADF abducted thirty girls and three boys from Mitandi Secondary School outside Fort Portal.

On June 9, 1998, the ADF attempted a similar mass abduction of students from the Kichwamba Technical School in Kasese district. When the students heard the rebels coming, they attempted to resist by locking themselves in their dormitories. The ADF rebels doused three of the dormitories with gasoline and torched them, killing an estimated fifty to eighty students who were trapped inside. The bodies were burned beyond recognition, making identification and an accurate death toll difficult. The rebels then retreated into the Rwenzori mountains with an estimated one hundred abductees, including students and civilians. An additional ten bodies were found in the region over the next days, including several civilians and a student, as well as two UPDF soldiers who were reportedly beheaded.

The Movement System and Conflict

A common theme among the many rebel groups operating in Uganda is that they are fighting against what they characterize as a dictatorial government imposed by President Museveni. Peter Otia, leader of the presently inactive rebel movement the Uganda People's Army (UPA), recently claimed his movement is fighting for a return to democracy in Uganda:

> Today, in the constitution, Ugandans are denied the basic and fundamental right of freedom of association. NRM is a totalitarian regime under the control of one man. When you have a leader of a

political party which is synonymous with the state, and is also the president, defense minister and in charge of all security organs, you are creating a garrison.... We are fighting for the restoration of democracy.[317]

In a public meeting in London in June 1998, representatives of the LRA's political wing, the Lords Resistance Movement (LRM), similarly claimed that the LRA was fighting against political oppression in Uganda. According to LRM spokesperson David Masanga, the LRA is fighting to overthrow Museveni's "dictatorship" and to establish a multiparty system in Uganda: "We oppose Article 269 of the constitution banning political parties... We are fighting a war for freedom of conscience in Uganda, fighting for the enjoyment of fundamental human rights and freedoms of every person in Uganda. We cannot talk peace when there is no freedom."[318] The Allied Democratic Forces (ADF) rebel group have similarly claimed to be fighting against what they perceive to be the one-party state established by President Museveni.

Such statements should be evaluated in the context of the conduct of these rebel groups, as well as their general inability to establish a popular basis of civilian support. The human rights abuses committed by the LRA and ADF are severe, and do not match the causes they ascribe to their rebellion: both have been responsible for a campaign of terror against the civilian population in their areas of operation. Robert Gersony, an independent consultant who carried out a field study of the conflict in the north for the U.S. Agency for International Development (USAID) concluded that popular support for the LRA is minimal:

Of the Acholi people in Gulu and Kitgum, more than ninety percent do not respect, welcome, encourage, support or voluntarily assist the LRA. The proportion of those who repudiate its conduct and continuation of the conflict is probably even higher in Kitgum than in Gulu. ... The attitude of the Acholi people appears to have evolved from enthusiastic support for the UPDA and Alice Lakwena; to skepticism during the Severino [Alice Lakwena's father] and early Kony period; to total opposition during the current LRA period, characterized by bitter anguish over what they fear is the "disappearance of the Acholi people." ... Repudiation of the LRA should not be construed as support for the

---

[317]"UPA to resume war against NRM—Otai," *Monitor*, July 31, 1998.
[318]Statement by David Masanga, LRM representative, Institute for African Alternatives, London, June 27, 1998.

current government. The National Resistance Movement and President Museveni are seen as alien to the area. While support for the armed anti-government struggle has evaporated, the population's political opposition to the current government remains.[319]

All of the persons interviewed by Human Rights Watch in the North expressed strong opposition to the current LRA campaign, and many called upon Kony to abandon his armed struggle and "come home."

Both the ADF and LRA have engaged in a systematic disinformation campaign which aims to avoid accountability for their atrocities and clearly exaggerates the scope of Ugandan army abuses. For example, at a June 1998 meeting attended by Human Rights Watch, LRA spokesperson Steven Nyeko claimed that the UPDF (the Ugandan army), not the LRA, was responsible for massacres and other abuses in the north, and claimed international human rights organizations were relying on "government propaganda" when accusing the LRA of abuses. Nyeko went on to claim that the LRA did not abduct the 139 girls en masse from the St. Mary's School in Aboke, a particularly notorious case documented in prior Human Rights Watch reports,[320] but rather evacuated them because the LRA "knew government troops would come and rape them."[321] Such attempts at disinformation are clearly at odds with the evidence established by independent observers, the press, and international human rights monitors.

The ADF has engaged in similar disinformation campaigns, blaming attacks for which it has been responsible on the UPDF and arguing that it does not abduct civilians but merely protects them from UPDF abuse. In a statement faxed to Human Rights Watch in the aftermath of an ADF massacre at Kichwamba, in

---

[319]Gersony, *The Anguish of Northern Uganda*, p.259-63. The historical development of the northern rebellion is discussed below.

[320]See Human Rights Watch, *The Scars of Death* (1997). Human Rights Watch collected more than one hundred testimonials from Aboke girls who were abducted during this incident and later released, and reprinted some of these letters in the report. The testimonies clearly establish that the girls were forcibly abducted by the LRA. For example, one girl wrote: "It was on October 9, 1996 when the Kony rebels appeared to break into our school. They entered the school by breaking the windows of our dormitory and then managed to enter the dormitory and open the door. They came in and switched on the lights. All of us were caught and tied up with ropes and [we] walked with them all night until we reached a certain far village." Ibid., p. 87.

[321]Statement by Steve Nyeko, LRM representative, Institute for African Alternative, London, June 27, 1998.

which an estimated eighty students were burned to death, the ADF advanced such a theory:

> In many cases after engaging the army and defeating it, we withdraw then after some hours the army comes in with a lot of force pouncing on civilians out of great anger and desperation due to the beating given to their fellow soldiers and kill, maim or even burn houses.... On realising these occurrences, the civilian population always pleads with the rebel fighters to take them to avoid the Government army wrath.[322]

Again, as with the LRA denials, such ADF statements are in direct contradiction to the evidence from eyewitnesses and victims interviewed by Human Rights Watch and other organizations. Human Rights Watch interviewed numerous persons in the west who described being abducted by force or physically abused by the ADF rebel movement. Our interviews took place out of the presence of government representatives, and most witnesses interviewed were located by our own initiatives, not provided by a government source.[323] The LRA and ADF representatives' suggestion that the work of international human rights groups represents a biased, pro-government perspective is mistaken and an attempt to deflect criticism from their own appalling human rights records.

Despite these important reservations about the purported political motivations of Ugandan rebel groups, it would be a mistake to suggest that rebel activity is completely unrelated to the suppression of political opposition activity in Uganda. The movement system of government deprives nonviolent political opposition of some of its effectiveness because it does not allow organized political opposition. The frustration created by the ineffectiveness of peaceful avenues of political opposition was described by an international journalist:

> Unfortunately, [Museveni's] critics have nowhere to channel their criticism, except through individual members of parliament. Under Museveni's 'movement' system of government, political party activity is banned, because he believes it fosters sectarianism. Theoretically, opposition politicians are instead absorbed into a broad-based

---

[322]Press Release by Allied Democratic Movement/Army, signed by Chairman Ssengooba Kyakonye Mukongozzi, faxed to Human Rights Watch May 15, 1998.

[323]Some persons interviewed in detention facilities were of course under government control, but interviews with detainees took place outside the presence of any government observers.

government. In reality, Museveni's cabinet is full of his devotees. The movement is beginning to look less like an alternate form of democracy, and more like a benign version of a one-party state. Increasingly, people resent not being given the freedom to exercise their choice.[324]

Okello Okello, an opposition member of parliament for the northern district of Kitgum, expressed his concerns to Human Rights Watch that the movement system in Uganda would inevitably lead to violent conflict:

> I am an old man. I have served in all the independence governments as a civil servant, as a land appraiser. In my twenty-six years of government service, I have seen many governments come and go.

> In Uganda, it is not yet *uhuru* [freedom] the way things are. I think we are sitting on a time bomb, and it will be terrible when it explodes. What we have now is an effective one-party state, even a baby can see this. They want to use state funds to run a political party. You cannot have a political organization in which membership is by birth. This to me is a deceptive scheme designed purposely to perpetuate governance by a small clique. The actual ruling clique is quite small, with the rest of us serving as window-dressing. But people are beginning to learn that they have been tricked. This system is a declaration of future war. When you close all avenues of opposition, where do you want them to go? They will go back to the gun, obviously. There will be a time when they can't take it no more.[325]

Professor Mamdani of the University of Cape Town has suggested that the prohibition on an effective opposition to the NRM government has escalated political differences into military differences, stating that "failure to allow peaceful avenues for organized opposition tends to turn opposition into a violent affair."[326] Professor Mamdani's argument finds some support in the historical record of rebel movements in Uganda. Among the different factions which form the ADF, for example, are Buganda federalists (advocates for the *federo* system which would return Buganda to the semi-autonomous status it enjoyed at independence) and

---

[324]Anna Borzello, "The Charmer," *BBC Focus on Africa*, August 1998.
[325]Human Rights Watch interview with Okello Okello, MP (Kitgum district), Kampala, April 14, 1998.
[326]"Political Party Ban Threatens Uganda—Professor," Reuters, July 5, 1998.

multipartyist who turned to armed opposition after their proposals for a federal, multiparty system were rejected at the 1995 Constituent Assembly. Former Democratic Party treasurer Evaristo Nyanzi and renegade UPDF officers Major Fred Mpiso and Major Herbert Itongwa are some of the figures who attempted to form the National Democratic Army (NDA) rebel group in Buganda following the rejection of federalist and multiparty proposals at the Constituent Assembly, and elements of the now defunct NDA have been incorporated into the ADF.[327] Another component of the ADF rebellion, drawn from radical elements within the Tabliq Muslim community, may have turned to armed resistance after their Islamic party, the Uganda Islamic Revolutionary Party, was banned on the grounds that it violated the constitutional prohibition on religiously based and other "sectarian" political organizations.

In the view of many Ugandans, the political restrictions of the movement system are also an obstacle to peace. There appears to be widespread support for peace talks among the civilian population, church leadership, and civil society. But the movement system has not allowed for the effective political mobilization of these sentiments to serve as a counterweight to the views of President Museveni and UPDF leaders, who have maintained a public commitment to a military solution despite the views of many analysts that the army lacks the motivation or capacity to achieve a military victory.   In the context of these dynamics, it is difficult to completely divorce the rebellions in northern and western Uganda from the political system in place in Uganda.

---

[327]Henry Gombya and Odoobo C. Bichachi, "Maj. Mpiso swears to fight Museveni," *Monitor*, July 7, 1997.

VIII. ARBITRARY PRE-TRIAL DETENTION: THE ABUSE OF TREASON AND OTHER PUBLIC ORDER CHARGES

In addition to the widespread use of treason charges against those suspected of collaborating with the rebel movements active in Uganda, the NRM government has frequently used treason charges to detain a wide range of actual or perceived opponents of the NRM, even though conviction on treason charges carries a mandatory death sentence. Under the Ugandan Constitution, a person charged with treason or similar offenses which are only triable by the High Court must be released on bail "on such conditions as the court considers reasonable" if they have been on remand for 360 days. However, in some cases persons remain incarcerated on remand for periods as long as five years, in clear violation of their constitutional and international human rights.[328]

In other treason cases where the remand period has ended and treason suspects were released on the order of a court, police have circumvented the law by rearresting the suspects and bringing new treason charges based on the same information. This happened in May 1998, when eighteen suspected members of the West Nile Bank Front (WNBF) rebel groups were rearrested on the same treason charges immediately after a court ordered their release because they had served more than 360 days (the maximum period allowed) awaiting trial on remand.[329] Twenty-seven ADF suspects who were freed on bond in May 1998 because they had spent more than one year in prison on remand were similarly rearrested.[330]

In an interview with Human Rights Watch just days after the release and rearrest of the WNBF suspects, Major General Salim Saleh expressed his strong disagreement with the release of the WNBF suspects, claiming that the released suspects had been selected out from a larger group of WNBF captives "because they cannot be reformed," and suggesting that the released rebel suspects would flee. The major-general further justified continued detention by arguing that the

---

[328]Human Rights Watch interview with Constantine Karusoke, Commissioner, Human Rights Commission, Kampala, April 8, 1998. Amnesty International has also documented cases of persons who remained on remand for treason charges for almost four years. Amnesty International, *Uganda: The Failure to Safeguard Human Rights* (London: Amnesty International, 1992), p. 47.

[329]Wamboga-Mugirya and Patrick Ongom Komakech, "WBNF 'rebels' back in jail," *Monitor*, April 30, 1998, p. 6; Edith Kimuli, "WNBF chiefs set for trial," *New Vision*, May 6, 1998, p. 7.

[330]"27 ADF suspects re-arrested," *New Vision*, May 23, 1998.

government was at least respecting the WNBF suspects' right to life: "As long as they are alive, it is a better situation. They will get out eventually."[331]

Law Professor Jjuuko of Makerere University placed the use of treason charges in a larger history of detention without trial in Uganda:

> The government right from 1986 has used treason charges in unprecedented numbers. At first, many of the cases were against Buganda monarchists and other dissidents. Now it is almost all people from the North and the West Nile region. Some are peasants, others are political dissidents. The treason charges arose out of pressure from human rights groups objecting to the long-term detention of persons at military barracks, a practice known as "lodging." In 1987 and 1988, the constitution was amended to allow the president to declare a state of emergency, and to allow for special military courts in those areas under a state of emergency. When this didn't work, they resorted to treason charges, basically using them as holding charges. In other countries, treason is only used in the context of war but in Uganda the charge has been almost routine. But in most cases they will not prosecute them, they are holding charges because bail can only be granted after one year. This makes the right to a speedy trial meaningless.[332]

Torture, Coerced Confessions, and Treason Charges

In April 1998, Human Rights Watch investigated the cases of a group of incarcerated treason suspects accused of involvement in the ADF rebellion in Western Uganda, conducting interviews with many of the suspects, the police officer in charge of the investigations, the magistrate monitoring the cases, local community leaders, and prison officials. The evidence gathered paints a disturbing picture. At the time of our visit to the regional Mubuku prison work farm, there were sixty-four persons on remand on treason charges, and four persons on remand for the lesser charge of misprision or concealment of treason.[333]

---

[331]Human Rights Watch interview with Major General Salim Saleh, overseer, Ministry of Defense, Gulu, April 25, 1998.

[332]Human Rights Watch interview with Frederick Jjuuko, Makerere University Law Professor, Kampala, April 14, 1998.

[333]Human Rights Watch interview with Amos Turyashaba, Deputy Officer-in-Command, Mubuku Government Prison Farm, April 21, 1998. According to the Uganda Penal Code, concealment or misprision of treason is committed by "any person who knowing that any person intends to commit treason does not give information thereof with

Most of the suspects were arrested by either the army or by internal security officers (known as DISO, district internal security officers). Several suspects claimed they were tortured at the army barracks at Kabukero where soldiers put sticks between their fingers, tied their hands together and then beat down on their hands with stones.[334] A number of the suspects claimed that they had been tied to a tree and had been brutally beaten by soldiers with a heavy cane, and showed Human Rights Watch the deep cuts on their buttocks which they said were the result of the beatings.[335] One of the suspects told Human Rights Watch that he witnessed soldiers torturing another suspect by burning a jerry can and dripping the burning plastic on his exposed skin.[336] The purpose of the torture was apparently to extract evidence which was then used to arrest other suspects and repeat the same procedures:

> They beat me for about ten minutes on the hands, and then I had to accept that I knew something about the rebels. If they asked you who you were collaborating with, you must just say any name of a person you can think of. I had to identify three people. There were two boys who had been detained by the army for long, and they told us that if we did not cooperate we would die. We had no choice. The two boys gave the same names which I should mention [to the interrogators].[337]

After reportedly forcing the suspects to identify other suspects and make confessions through torture, the army brought the suspects to the police. Because confessions extracted by the army are not admissible as evidence, the army officers took the suspects to a location outside the barracks, where the detainees said they were met by police officers and forced to sign admissions while surrounded by

---

all reasonable dispatch to the Minister, an administrative officer, a magistrate or an officer in charge of a police station, or use all reasonable endeavours to prevent the commission of the offense of treason." Uganda Penal Code, section 27.

[334]Human Rights Watch interviews with suspects 1, 2, 3, 6, Mubuku Government Prison Farm, April 21, 1998.

[335]Human Rights Watch interviews with suspects 2, 5, 6, Mubuku Government Prison Farm, April 21, 1998.

[336]Human Rights Watch interviews with suspect 3, Mubuku Government Prison Farm, April 21, 1998.

[337]Human Rights Watch interviews with suspect 6, Mubuku Government Prison Farm, April 21, 1998.

army soldiers.[338] These admissions, in some cases dictated by the military, are the basis for their continued incarceration on treason charges.

The police, who are supposed to investigate and charge suspects, seemed intimidated by the army and barely carried out investigations, claiming it was impossible to reach the areas and gather witnesses. Police officials freely admitted to Human Rights Watch that they were operating in an "arrest now, investigate later" mode. In fact, it appeared that even after arrest no substantial investigations were taking place. Moses Otwili, the chief investigations officer (CID) for the Kasese District, told Human Rights Watch that it is possible that many of the suspects were innocent: "You may find that some people are innocent but we cannot release them. Otherwise the soldiers will think we are collaborators."[339] Otwili continued:

> We just charged some people from Kichwamba with treason. Some may be innocent, but there is no time to gather evidence of their innocence. You can get arrested for nothing and there is nothing that you can do about it. We feel sorry for them, but it is like catching a stray bullet in a war zone.[340]

One of the suspects was crying when he told Human Rights Watch of the suffering of his wife and ten children since they were deprived of their only breadwinner. Another suspect told Human Rights Watch that he was responsible for a total of nineteen children since the death of his brother, and that five of these children and his brother's wife had died from hunger and disease since his incarceration.[341]

As in western Uganda, the UPDF frequently arrests people in the north on suspicion of being rebels, detaining them illegally at their barracks before turning them over to the police without any information:

> The arresting soldiers tended to leave [the police station] without recording statements or leaving their contact address. Such people then remained in detention at the police station. Although they did not admit

---

[338]Human Rights Watch interviews with suspects 1, 2, 5, 6, Mubuku Government Prison Farm, April 21, 1998.

[339]Human Rights Watch interview with Moses Otwili, Assistant Superintendent (CID), Kasese police station, Kasese, April 24, 1998.

[340]Ibid.

[341]Human Rights Watch interviews with suspect 5, Mubuku Government Prison Farm, April 21, 1998.

it, the police appeared to keep the suspects in detention in fear of annoying the UPDF. They could not take the detainees to court because they had no facts on which to base a charge.[342]

The investigation of one series of treason cases strongly supports the view that treason charges are being used in Uganda as a "holding charge," effectively neutralizing political opponents, dissidents, and other suspected persons on the flimsiest of charges. James Otto, secretary-general of Gulu-based Human Rights Focus, told Human Rights Watch that "treason charges are used as a holding charge, in the same way that Obote used detention orders."[343] In the words of an earlier Amnesty International report, "the charge of treason...has been used to hold suspected opponents despite the absence of sufficient evidence on which to base a prosecution, let alone a conviction."[344]   The number of persons on remand for treason in Uganda as of September 1998 exceeds 1,000. Some of the cases involve a large number of suspects: 114 people have remained on remand for treason at Luzira prison following a UPDF raid on a Tabliq rebel training camp near Buseruka, Hoima district, in August 1995. In December 1998, more than 600 treason suspects detained at Luzira prison, most of them arrested in the West Nile region during 1997, wrote to President Museveni to request a presidential pardon. The group claimed that out of their original group of 650 suspects, fifty-two had died between January and April 1998 at Luzira prison from various ailments.[345] Unconscionably long remand times are not only a feature of treason charges, but characterize almost all serious charges in Uganda, pointing to serious deficiencies in the administration of justice.   For example, the Uganda Human Rights Commission has documented the case of Frenjo Olima, who was arrested in Arua on a murder charge in 1984. He was acquitted in 1991 on the charge, but was sent back to prison by the state attorney. The HRC found that he was still in detention in 1997: "Neither he nor the prison authorities knew why he was there."[346]

---

[342]Uganda Human Rights Commission, *1997 Report*, para 3.13, p. 17.

[343]Human Rights Watch interview with James Otto, Secretary-General, Human Rights Focus, Gulu, April 28, 1998.

[344]Amnesty International, *Uganda: The Failure to Safeguard Human Rights* (London: Amnesty International, 1992), p. 47.

[345]Moses Draku, "Uganda Treason Suspects Beg for Pardon," *Pan-African News Service*, December 24, 1998.

[346]Uganda Human Rights Commission, *1997 Report*, para 4.41, p. 31.

Abuse of Treason Charges as a Method of Political Control
   The almost unchecked power of the UPDF to arrest and incarcerate civilians
has created a climate of political repression. Especially in the rural areas
destabilized by rebel conflicts, persons are fearful to express and advocate political
beliefs at odds with the NRM out of fear of being identified as rebel sympathizers.
Cecilia Ogwal told Human Rights Watch, "Treason charges are normally used in
areas of insurgency. They pick key activists from among the multipartyists or
people opposed to the government and frame them as collaborators with the
rebels."[347] Wycliffe Birungi, chairperson of the human rights committee of the
Uganda Law Society, shared a similar view with Human Rights Watch:

> Offenses such as treason are normally used by the state to stifle dissent
> or opposition, especially against political opponents. Some of these
> political opponents are nonviolent, but there are also many who are
> captured in the rebel zones and charged with terrorism.... In almost all
> of these cases, the persons are innocent, but it is an effective way of
> suppressing any likely opposition. In most cases, the police doesn't even
> carry out investigations before it arrests these people. In an area like
> Arua, given there has been instability, I am of the opinion that the
> government does this to pacify and intimidate the population and to
> scare off opposition.[348]

   A number of prominent politicians have been charged with treason since the
NRM came to power. In May 1992, Zachary Olum, the organizing secretary of the
DP, Ojok Mulozi, the publicity secretary of the DP, and Tiberio Atwoma Okeny,
chairman of the National Liberal Party, were acquitted of treason after the judge
concluded that the "whole trial was politically motivated."[349] The case had
originally involved eighteen prominent leaders from the north arrested in March
and April 1991, including the minister of state for foreign affairs, Daniel Omara
Atubo, and cases were either dismissed or resulted in acquittal. In January 1992,
Robert Kitariko, secretary-general of the DP, and Ojok Mulozi, publicity secretary
of the DP, and others were charged with treason in a related case. Their case was

---

[347]Human Rights Watch interview with Cecilia Ogwal, Chairperson, Interim Executive
Committee of the UPC, Kampala, April 13, 1998.
   [348]Human Rights Watch interview with Wycliffe Birungi, Chairperson, Human Rights
Committee of the Uganda Law Society, Kampala, April 10, 1998.
   [349]Amnesty International, *Uganda: The Failure to Safeguard Human Rights* (London:
Amnesty International, 1992), p. 46.

dismissed in March 1992, and Kitariko is currently a member of the Electoral Commission.

Brigadier Moses Ali, a former Uganda National Rescue Front (UNRF) leader and at the time the minister of youth, culture and sport in Museveni's government, was arrested in April 1990 on treason charges. He remained incarcerated for twenty-six months until his acquittal in June 1992, with the judge commenting that the prosecution evidence was "unreliable and worthless."[350] Moses Ali is currently second deputy prime minister and minister of tourism, trade and industry. In March 1994, two UPC leaders were arrested and charged with sedition for publishing a revised party manifesto which claimed that Uganda was ruled by Tutsis.[351]

Joseph Lusse, a prominent Kampala business man and staunch DP supporter, has been repeatedly charged with treason, first in 1988 and again in 1995. On October 30, 1998, Lusse and his six co-defendants were acquitted by High Court Justice Patrick Tabaro, who stated that there was no evidence to support the treason charges. However, Lusse was rearrested immediately after his acquittal, and has again been remanded to prison on the basis of identical treason charges. During a recent court appearance, Lusse reportedly told the presiding justice that he had been tortured while in custody, and removed some of his clothes to show the scars he claimed were caused by torture.[352]

Although the use of treason charges against prominent politicians has diminished in recent years, the overbroad use of treason charges affects the ability and willingness of local activists, especially in rebel areas, to criticize the government.

In March 1998, nine northerners were arrested around Gulu and later charged with treason by Major Kakooza-Mutale, a presidential advisor on political affairs. The arrests were strongly criticized by Northern politicians, including the Acholi parliamentary group, the Gulu RDC, and the Minister of State Resident in the North as an unconstitutional exercise of power.[353] One of the persons arrested was Okello Layoo, the just-elected chairperson of the LC III council for Anaka subcounty in Nwoya county. The frequent resort to treason charges and lengthy

[350]Ibid., p. 51.
[351]Amnesty International, *Attacks on Human Rights Through the Misuse of Criminal Charges* (London: Amnesty International, 1995).
[352]"Lusse Acquitted, Remanded," *New Vision*, October 3, 1998.
[353]Christopher Ojera, "Maj. Kakooza's arrests anger minister Dollo," *Monitor*, May 1, 1998; John Muto-Ono p'Lajur, "Gulu RDC attacks Museveni adviser," *Monitor*, April 6, 1998; Emmy Allio and Eric Lakidi, "Acholi MPs shun Kakooza," *New Vision*, May 9, 1998.

incarcerations, when viewed together with the army's outspoken support for the NRM, makes for a repressive and chilling climate.

Use of Treason Charges Against Children

Treason charges are not only applied to silence political opponents and dissidents, they are also used against those suspected of collaboration with the rebel movements, including children. Children—defined internationally as those under the age of eighteen—have been charged with treason because of their alleged involvement with rebel groups in the north and west of Uganda. These groups, most notably the LRA, ADF, and WNBF, have engaged in frequent abductions of children, often forcing them to join their ranks as combatants. Used as pawns in a conflict that has little to do with them, the children may now find themselves facing the most serious of criminal charges. Children charged with treason have been detained for long periods of time, confined with adults in army barracks or police cells, and subject to torture and abuse.

Although Ugandan law considers treason to be a capital offense, the death penalty may not be imposed upon those below the age of eighteen at the time of the offense.[354] Children who are accused of capital crimes may be held no longer than six months on remand.[355] If a child's case is not completed one year after he or she is formally charged, it must be dismissed and the child absolved of any future liability for the alleged offense.[356]

Although codified in Ugandan law, in practice these juvenile justice standards are frequently ignored. According to the Ugandan Children's Statute, the cases of children accused of capital crimes must be heard by the High Court rather than by the investigative, child-focused Family and Children Court. The law mandates that the High Court, when hearing juvenile cases, "shall have due regard to the child's age and to the provisions of the law relating to the procedures for trials involving children."[357] Unfortunately, implementation of this provision has been frustrated by limited resources and by the reluctance of many officials to accord special treatment to children accused of serious crimes.[358]

Due to poor record keeping within Uganda's juvenile justice system, it is difficult to confirm the number of children detained for treason. In January 1998,

---

[354]Trial on Indictments Decree 26 of 1971, Section 104(1).

[355]Children's Statute, Sections 89 and 91 (6) (a).

[356]Children's Statute, Section 100 (4).

[357]Children's Statute, Section 105 (3).

[358]Human Rights Watch email correspondence with Diane M. Swales, National Social Welfare Advisor, Save the Children Fund-UK, September 7, 1998.

---

the Ugandan Human Rights Commission found that twenty-five children were held at Naguru Remand Home on charges of treason. Seventeen had been arrested in the West Nile Region and accused of fighting with the WNBF against the Ugandan government. Eight were arrested in Kasese and were accused of collaborating with ADF rebels.[359] Confidential sources claim that most of these children have been released, but several continue to be held on treason charges while other children have since been arrested on similar charges. The Foundation for Human Rights Initiative established that forty children were being held on treason charges in Jinja prison during a September, 1998, visit to the facility. The children were brought to Jinja prison from Arua (West Nile) in May 1997, where they were allegedly involved in WNBF rebel activities. Some of the cases were committed to the High Court in June 1998.[360] The outcome of the cases and the whereabouts of the other children is unknown to Human Rights Watch. They were between ten and sixteen years old at the time of their arrival at Jinja prison. It is likely that other children are being detained at different prisons, as well as at military facilities.

Many children who have surrendered or escaped from rebel forces have been detained in army barracks or police cells for interrogation, where they are usually confined with adults, in violation of their rights under Ugandan and international law.[361] Human Rights Watch was told by army sources in Kasese that children are routinely kept at army barracks for "debriefing," and it appears that the army continues to detain children and other civilians for unspecified periods of time with little oversight, a practice know as "lodging" which used to be widespread. For example, Human Rights Watch interviewed three young men at Mbarara barracks who had been in detention for several months, apparently because the army wanted to use them to identify ADF collaborators. Such suspected rebel collaborators who

---

[359]UNICEF Report, "Children Charged with Treason: Brief Update Note," March 20, 1998.

[360]Letter from Livingstone Sewanyana, Executive Director of the Foundation for Human Rights Initiative (FHRI), to Human Rights Watch, dated September 24, 1998.

[361]UNICEF Report, "Children Charged with Treason: Brief Update Note," March 20, 1998; Commissioner C.K. Karusoke, "Children Under Treason Charge Being Kept at Naguru Remand Home," May 29, 1997, materials on file with Human Rights Watch. International and national laws state that juveniles in detention must be separated from adults. ICCPR, Article 10 (2) (b); Convention on the Rights of the Child, Article 37 (c); U.N. Rules for the Protection of Juveniles Deprived of Their Liberty, Rule 29; U.N. Standard Minimum Rules for the Administration of Juvenile Justice, Rule 10.1; Ugandan Children's Statute, Section 90 (8); U.N. Standard Minimum Rules for the Treatment of Prisoners, Rule 85 (2).

are kept in extrajudicial detention at army barracks for the purpose of identifying other rebel suspects are commonly referred to as "computers" by army personnel.

The unwillingness of the army to grant human rights investigators adequate access to its facilities in order to investigate charges of illegal detentions at army barracks makes it difficult to establish the overall level of such abuses. The Uganda Human Rights Commission (HRC) is constitutionally empowered to visit all places of detention, but the UPDF has refused to respect this provision and insists that the HRC give notice and seek permission before visiting any military facilities. Such permission was denied when the HRC sought to visit military barracks in Gulu and Kasese.[362] Requiring human rights monitors to seek such prior permission deprives the monitors of an element of surprise, and may allow the UPDF to temporarily "clean up" problems prior to the visit by moving detainees to other facilities. In 1997, the UPDF granted the HRC permission to visit four different UPDF facilities around Kampala, and the HRC found civilians in detention at all four of these facilities. The UPDF sought to justify these detentions on the basis of the National Resistance Army Statute of 1992, which allows the UPDF to subject civilians to military law under certain conditions.[363] The National Resistance Army Statute, which is interpreted by UPDF as allowing for indefinite detention, is inconsistent with the 1995 constitution and international law.

UNICEF representatives, working with the Gulu Support the Children (GUSCO) and World Vision trauma centers, have been able to negotiate a relatively rapid release process for most children who flee from the LRA and find their way into UPDF custody. According to officials at the trauma centers, most children are released to the trauma centers by UPDF within less than a week, although some children may be kept longer if they are deemed to have valuable intelligence information. There are now "child rights" liaison desks established at the UPDF central barracks in the north, with staff assigned to expedite the departure of children from the barracks. These desks were recently established in Gulu, Arua, Kitgum, Adjumani and Moyo UPDF barracks.[364] However, it appears that in some cases, especially where the UPDF feels they have captured what they consider to be an actual rebel—as opposed to an abducted child who escaped from LRA custody—children are kept longer.

---

[362]Uganda Human Rights Commission, *1997 Report*, para 3.19, p. 18.

[363]Ibid, para 3.13, p. 17 and para 4.43-44, p. 31.

[364]Human Rights Watch email correspondence with Leila Pakkala, Information/Advocacy Officer, UNICEF Uganda Country Office, October 7, 1998.

Amy, who was seventeen at the time of her interview with Human Rights Watch in April 1998, was abducted by the LRA from Kitgum district in October 1995, and marched to Sudan for military training. In April 1996, according to her account, she returned to Uganda with a 400-strong contingent of LRA rebels. During an ambush at Pajule, she was captured in June 1996 by UPDF, who considered her a captured rebel and not an escapee from the LRA. She was kept at Pajule barracks for four days, and repeatedly beaten by UPDF soldiers. She was then taken to Kitgum barracks, where she was kept for three weeks: "It was very hot during the day and we were starving because there was not enough food. We did not get enough water, and sometimes had to stay for days without water. When you get one cup of water, it is supposed to last you two days." She was then brought to Gulu barracks, where she was kept for another two weeks together with another woman who had spent six years with the LRA. In August 1996, the two were brought to Lubiri barracks near Kampala, together with three male suspected LRA rebels. According to Amy, the three male suspects, Anthony Langol, Richard Ojara and Robert Otim, were severely beaten and received electric shocks at Lubiri. She believed that the three men were later killed by the UPDF at Lubiri barracks, an allegation which could not be independently confirmed by Human Rights Watch. Amy and the other woman were locked inside a darkened room for a long period, and then had to remain at Lubiri for several more months. She was finally released to one of the trauma centers in May 1997, nearly a year after she was originally captured.[365]

Some children have been detained for months before being formally charged and committed to remand. Eight children who were suspected of involvement in ADF rebel activities were held in the Kampala Central Police Station for more than nine months without ever being taken to court.[366] Five of the children's families had not been notified of their arrests.[367] One child was only seven years old, five

---

[365]Human Rights Watch interview, Gulu, April 28, 1998.

[366]UNICEF Report, "Children Charged with Treason: Brief Update Note," 20 March 1998. Section 90 (3) of the Children's Statute states that "where release on bond is not granted, a child shall be detained in police custody for a maximum of twenty-four hours or until the child is taken before a court, whichever is sooner."

[367]Commissioner C.K. Karusoke, "Children Under Treason Charge Being Kept at Naguru Remand Home," 29 May 1997. Section 90 (3) of the Children's Statute provides that "where a child is arrested by the police, his/her parents or guardians...shall be informed." See also Convention on the Rights of the Child, Article 37 (c); U.N. Rules for the Protection of Juveniles Deprived of Their Liberty, Rule 59; U.N. Standard Minimum Rules for the Administration of Juvenile Justice, Rule 13.4.

years below the age of criminal responsibility.[368] According to a representative of Save the Children Fund UK (SCF-UK), child returnees are also regularly detained in Kasese police cells for interrogation.[369]

Although children charged with capital crimes are supposed to be committed to juvenile remand homes for a period not exceeding six months, in practice, some children have remained incarcerated on remand for as long as two years.[370] According to a May 1997 Ugandan Human Rights Commission (HRC) report, Mutebi Ali, aged eighteen, had been detained for two years before he was taken away by ADF rebels during a prison breakout in February 1998.[371] Dramadri Swadek, sixteen, had been in detention since his arrest in May 1996, spending two months in Koboko barracks and a year in Makingye barracks before being charged with treason and sent to Naguru Remand Home.[372]

Some of the children and young people detained on treason charges in Naguru Remand Center claim that they were physically abused while in army barracks or police cells.[373] In 1997, Ahamed Bugembe, then aged eighteen, Sulaiman Ssemwogerere, eighteen, and Hamad Sebuliba, fourteen, told a HRC commissioner that they had been tortured while interrogators demanded that they explain their

---

[368]Section 89 of the Convention on the Rights of the Child sets the minimum age of criminal responsibility at 12 years.

[369]Diane M. Swales, email correspondence, September 7, 1998.

[370]Diane M. Swales, email correspondence, September 7, 1998. Article 10 (2) (b) of the ICCPR, Article 40 (2) (b) (iii) of the CRC, and Rule 17 of the Beijing Rules require states to adjudicate juvenile cases as quickly as possible. In October 1997, the Committee on the Rights of the Child expressed concern about the "administration of juvenile justice [in Uganda]...in particular, violations of the rights of children in detention centers, the remanding of children in adult prisons or police cells, long periods in custody, and the inadequacy of existing alternative measures to imprisonment." CRC/15/Add. 80.

[371]The ages given in the report cited are the children's ages at the time of their interview with Commissioner C.K. Karusoke of the Ugandan Human Rights Commission on May 29, 1997. Commissioner C.K. Karusoke, "Children Under Treason Charge Being Kept at Naguru Remand Home," May 29, 1997.

[372]Commissioner C.K Karusoke, "Children Under Treason Charge," p. 5. According to the Ugandan Children's Code, these cases should have been dismissed one year after the children were formally charged with treason.

[373]Commissioner C.K. Karusoke, "Children Under Treason Charge." Article 37 (a) of the CRC sets out the right to be free from "torture or other cruel, inhuman, or degrading treatment or punishment." This right is also guaranteed by article 7 of the ICCPR, and by the Convention Against Torture and Other Cruel, Inhuman, or Degrading Treatment or Punishment.

presence at a mosque. Maliki Alias, sixteen, reported to the HRC that he was beaten every day while held in Ologa army barracks.[374]

UNICEF, Save the Children Fund (UK, Denmark, and Norway), and the Uganda Human Rights Commission have expressed their concern over the treatment of children detained on treason charges and have brought the issue to the attention of the Ugandan government on numerous occasions and at the highest levels. While the Office of the Director of Public Prosecutions has been responsive to appeals on behalf of particular detainees, it has not made a comprehensive effort to address the problem of the illegal detention and treatment of children accused of treason.[375]

---

[374]Commissioner C.K. Karusoke, "Children Under Treason Charge."
[375]Diane Swales, email correspondence, September 7, 1998.

IX. THE ROLE OF THE INTERNATIONAL COMMUNITY

Old Wine in New Bottles: The Shortcomings of the "New Leaders" Model

The debate over the movement system is not simply about the movement system in Uganda: it is about the future of democratization and respect for political rights in Sub-Saharan Africa in general. The restrictions on political rights which characterize the movement system of government are becoming increasingly common in the larger region, and President Museveni is aggressively marketing his movement system as an alternative to "alien" democratic models in Africa. When President Kabila of the Democratic Republic of Congo suspended political party activity in May 1997, President Museveni rallied to his side, stating: "I myself don't like political parties ... I restricted their activities. If Mr. Kabila copies that situation, I wouldn't be surprised."[376]

A number of hybrid governments have emerged in Africa which have stated a public commitment to economic reform and good governance, but which have resisted a return to multiparty democracy. Uganda, Ethiopia, Eritrea, and Rwanda are often mentioned as members of the club of "new" African governments, all led by relatively young and often charismatic guerrilla leaders turned statesmen.[377] These leaders claimed that the interest of stability required strong government, and that most African states were not ready for multiparty democracy until they developed a thriving economy and an established middle class. Restrictive political systems centered around a governing "movement" were characteristic of all these countries, and such a restrictive political system has legally developed to the greatest extent in Uganda. Despite claims to the contrary, the ideology of the movement appears to be leading towards a reinstatement of one-party rule, with the one difference that the "new leaders" not only tolerate but actively encourage private enterprise. The "new leaders" share a common suspicion of political

---

[376]"Mandela Accuses West of Demonizing Congo's Kabila," May 27, 1997.

[377]Scott Straus, "Africa's New Generation of Leaders," *Chronicle*; Scott Straus, Uganda the cradle of Modern Africa," *Globe and Mail* (Toronto); Demba Diallo and Corinne Moncel, "Ouganda: Une Réussite Paradoxale," *L'Autre Afrique*, May 28-June 3, 1997, pp. 84-86; Nicholas Kotch, "New Club of African Leaders the Event of 1997," Reuters, December 27, 1997; Johanna McGeary, "An African for Africa," *Time*, September 1, 1997, pp. 36-40; Philip Gourevitch, "Continental Shift," *New Yorker*, August 4, 1997, pp.42-55; Marina Ottaway, "Africa's 'New Leaders': African Solution or African Problem?," *Current History*, May 1998, pp. 209-213; Dan Connell and Frank Smyth, "Africa's New Bloc," *Foreign Affairs*, March/April 1998, pp. 95-106; Marina Ottaway, *Africa's New Leaders: Democracy or State Reconstruction* (New York: Carnegie Endowment for International Peace, 1999).

opposition activities, and have aggressively pursued their vision for a new Africa by intervening in the affairs of their neighbors through the sponsorship of rebel movements and, in the case of the former Zaire, through direct military intervention.[378] Because of the dramatic results which some of these leaders have produced in the area of economic reform and reduced political instability, the international community has often been willing to overlook the repressive measures these states have taken against perceived political opponents.

Beginning in 1997, the international community, led by the United States, embraced the leaders of Uganda, Eritrea, Ethiopia, Rwanda, and the DRC as the "new leaders" of Africa, painting them as advocates of strong government which were willing to bring "African solutions to African problems." The policies of the United States towards Africa became centered around these "new leaders" and the idea that this new leadership would lead an "African renaissance." In embracing these new leaders, the U.S. and other Western governments often overlooked serious and systematic human rights abuses committed by these governments. Repressive measures taken by these leaders against political opposition and civil society were often met with silence.

Flawed Engagement and Conspicuous Silence

The international community has been reluctant to call for democratic reform and respect for civil and political rights in Uganda, despite its often outspoken calls for similar reforms in neighboring countries, such as Kenya and the Democratic Republic of Congo. President Museveni is a popular leader in the international arena, and has shown his capacity as a power broker in the region on several occasions, such as by inviting a large number of African leaders to Kampala for a summit with President Clinton. Western countries and international monetary

---

[378]The Rwandan Patriotic Army (RPA) was based in Uganda for most of its guerrilla campaign which lasted from 1990 until 1994, and many RPA soldiers formerly served in Museveni's NRA. Uganda and Rwanda played a major role in the 1996-97 ADFL campaign which toppled Mobutu, and again sponsored and participated in a rebellion against Kabila which began in August 1998 when Kabila ordered his Rwandan military advisors to return to Rwanda. Zimbabwe, Angola and Namibia intervened militarily to support the Kabila government, and accused Uganda and Rwanda of invading the DRC. Uganda, Eritrea and Ethiopia have also provided extensive support to the SPLA. Sudan has justified its support for rebel groups in Uganda as retaliation for Museveni's support for the SPLA. Prunier, *The Rwanda Crisis;* Human Rights Watch, *What Kabila is Hiding*; John Pomfret, "Rwanda Planned and Led the Attack on Zaire," *Washington Post*, July 9, 1997; Human Rights Watch, "Sudan: Global Trade, Local Impact," *A Human Rights Watch Short Report*, vol. 10, no. 4(A) (August 1998).

institutions such as the World Bank and International Monetary Fund (IMF) appreciate Museveni's pragmatic economic management and rave about the positive economic growth rates in Uganda since the early nineties. Criticism of Museveni's NRM system by diplomats has been met with strong rebukes from Museveni, who likes to suggest that such critiques of his African solution are "not only meddling but meddling on the basis of ignorance, and, of course, some arrogance."[379] Most of the international community has chosen not to rock the boat, often turning a blind eye to restrictions on civil and political rights. In a country surrounded by such problematic countries as Sudan, Kenya, the Democratic Republic of Congo and Rwanda, the international community seems to accept the serious human rights abuses in Uganda as a minor issue, and has not engaged in much critical discussion with the Museveni government about these abuses.

The United States

The United States is one of the few donor nations which has attempted to engage in a substantial public discussion with the Museveni government about the movement system. The Museveni government is a close ally of the United States, as evidenced by the frequent high-level visits of U.S. officials to Uganda. Because of the close relationship between the U.S. and Uganda, U.S. criticism of the movement system has become increasingly muted. Many opposition politicians and advocates for pluralism in Uganda expressed concern to Human Rights Watch about the lack of engagement by the United States on the issue of political rights, and viewed recent comments and actions by the U.S. administration as an abandonment of their cause.

The U.S. took a more critical stance on the movement system during the 1995 constitutional debates. Noting the "undesirable, often tragic, consequences of governments which do not allow political competition and which deny human rights,"[380] the U.S. embassy in Kampala issued a strongly worded statement during the constitutional debates on Uganda's future political system:

> [D]espite the remarkable progress that Uganda has achieved, the United States now notes with concern that the stage is being set for the entrenchment of a system of government which falls seriously short of full democracy and political enfranchisement. Normally a constitution

---

[379]Philip Gourevitch, "Continental Shift," *New Yorker*, August 4, 1997, p. 50.
[380]Edmond Kizito, "U.S. urges Uganda to build full democracy," Reuters World Service, May 13, 1995.

is designed to protect human rights and ensure free and fair competition for political leadership. However, some forces in Uganda would like to see a constitution that preserves monopoly power indefinitely and continues the prohibition on the right of association and the right of assembly.[381]

President Museveni rejected the U.S. call for a speedy return to pluralist democracy, responding that "what the people of Uganda decide is what we shall take. It is not for the Americans to decide for Ugandans what is best for them."[382]

The U.S. embassy continued to periodically criticize the movement political system. In a July 1997 interview with the government's *New Vision* newspaper, outgoing U.S. ambassador Michael Southwick criticized the draft Movement and Political Organizations Bills then under consideration, accusing the drafters of aiming to "consolidate power in the hands of one group indefinitely."[383] Southwick went on to rule out any U.S. support for the scheduled year 2000 referendum on political parties: "You do not have a referendum on religious and press freedom, so why have it on freedom of association and assembly? These are not votable commodities."[384] The outgoing ambassador also questioned the credibility of the 1996 presidential and parliamentary elections, stating that, "Nobody should deceive themselves that these elections were free and fair in the sense that they met international norms. They should be seen as transitional elections."[385]

Recognizing the severe restrictions on opposition political party activity in Uganda, the State Department's country report for Uganda for 1997 explicitly refers to the movement system as a *one-party* system of government and bluntly states that "Movement domination of the political process limits the rights of citizens."[386] Yet official U.S. criticism of this has become noticeably muted. When Secretary of State Madeline Albright was asked during her 1997 visit to Uganda

---

[381] "U.S. warns that Kampala may fall 'short of full democracy,'" Deutsche Presse-Agentur, May 12, 1995.

[382] Edmond Kizito, "Uganda denies swift return to multiparty politics," Reuters World Service, May 18, 1995.

[383] Ofwono Opondo, "U.S. warns Uganda over referendum," *Sunday Vision*, July 20, 1997, p.1.

[384] Ibid.

[385] Ibid.

[386] U.S. Department of State Bureau of Democracy, Human Rights, and Labor, "Uganda Country Report on Human Rights Practices for 1997," (January 30, 1998).

whether she agreed with former Ambassador Southwick's call for multiparty democracy, her answer was evasive and did not take a position on the movement system, citing her admiration of Museveni's "progressive role and supportive role of democracy throughout the region."[387] During a pre-Clinton visit interview, Assistant Secretary of State for African Affairs, Susan Rice, seemed to endorse the idea of a referendum on Ugandans' right to free expression and association when she stated: "We all look forward to the year 2000 when the people of Uganda will make a free and open decision we hope about the form of political competition that they wish to see in their country. That's a decision for the people of Uganda."[388]

During the Clinton visit, U.S. Deputy Ambassador Michael McKinley organized a luncheon attended by U.S. Special Envoy for Democratization in Africa Rev. Jesse Jackson, Susan Rice, National Security Council (NSC) Director for Africa John Shattuck, and a number of other U.S. delegates. In addition to a number of movement-oriented members of the government, the luncheon guests included a number of well-known advocates of pluralism in Uganda and opposition politicians, including former presidential candidates Paul Ssemogerere (DP) and Muhammed Mayanja (Justice Forum); UPC members Cecilia Ogwal, Dr. James Rwanyarare, and Aggrey Awori; and Dr. Joe Oloka-Onyango of Makerere University. The luncheon was an important opportunity for U.S. policy makers to engage in a wide-ranging discussion on the Ugandan political climate with opposition politicians, and was perceived as a welcome message of solidarity with the cause of pluralism by some of the opposition politicians in attendance.[389] Rev. Jesse Jackson addressed the meeting, stating that although the U.S. did not have the

---

[387]The Secretary of State's answer was:
Well, first of all, let me say that we believe that the progress made in Uganda under President Museveni has been remarkable. We admire the work that he has done, and look forward to working with him in the future. I think that one of the messages that the United States always has as we travel around is that every country's human rights record can be improved, and that is true here also. We talked about this very briefly. My colleagues will pursue the subject, but I think the important thing to realize is that this country is a beacon in the Central African region, and we admire the work that the President has been doing here, on behalf of his own people as well as his very, I think progressive role and supportive role of democracy throughout the region.
[388]United States Information Agency, *Africa News Report*, March 23, 1998, p. 16.
[389]Human Rights Watch interview with U.S. embassy official, Kampala, May 6, 1998.

right to prescribe political systems to other countries, there were universal democratic principles which are a prerequisite for genuine governance.[390]

A press briefing during President Clinton's visit to Uganda offered an insight into the Clinton Administration's policy towards democratization and human rights in Uganda. The press briefing was addressed by Jesse Jackson, Susan Rice, and National Security Council (NSC) Director for Africa John Prendergast. Jesse Jackson strongly defended Uganda's movement system, arguing that it had been established by popular mandate, that Uganda was a democracy "more so than many other nations with which we have relations," and that democracy takes time to build. Susan Rice was more reserved, recognizing that "there is a long way to go" on democratization and human rights in Uganda, and stressing that respect for human rights was a fundamental benchmark for measuring democracy:

> The people of Uganda will ultimately choose the nature of their democratic system, whether it is multiparty or takes some other form. That's for them to decide. But in the meantime, we have made it absolutely clear and I think the government of Uganda fully shares the view that respect for basic human rights is fundamental and that democratic participation, freedom of expression, freedom of association—those have to be the benchmarks by which a democratic society is measured.[391]

But this linking of human rights and democracy has not been translated into a program of action. Bruised by past Museveni rejections of U.S. pressure, democratization and human rights no longer seem to occupy a high place on the U.S. agenda, despite the considerable leverage the U.S. and other donor states have because of their extensive activities in Uganda. While other governments in the region such as those of Kenya and Zambia become subjected to conditional funding which requires progress on democratization and human rights, the international community seems happy to continue with business as usual in Uganda. The lack of resolve is particularly disturbing in light of the extensive coverage that human right abuses in Uganda receive in the yearly U.S. State Department human rights

---

[390]Richard Mutumba, "U.S. Delegates Meet Opposition at Luncheon," *New Vision*, March 25, 1998.

[391]White House Press Briefing by U.S. Special Envoy for the Promotion of Democracy in Africa Reverend Jesse Jackson, National Security Council Director for Africa John Prendergast, Assistant Secretary of State for Africa Susan Rice, and USAID Administrator Brian Atwood, March 24, 1998.

reports. It is not that the U.S. is unaware of the political and human rights situation in Uganda: they simply have chosen to ignore it.

The Entebbe Joint Declaration of Principles signed by President Clinton and the heads of a number of African states during Clinton's Kampala visit was also seen as an implicit recognition of the movement system of government. Although the declaration recognized several core principles of democracy—the principles of inclusion, the rule of law, respect for human rights, the equality of all men and women, and the right of citizens to regularly elect their leaders freely and to participate fully in the decision-making which affects them—the declaration does not specifically recognize the rights which have been explicitly denied by the movement system. In addition, the declaration seems to accept Museveni's relativist arguments for limiting political rights when it recognizes that "there is no fixed model for democratic institutions or transformation."

A noted commentator on Ugandan politics, Professor Mahmood Mamdani of the University of Cape Town, questioned the priorities of the high-profile visit of President Clinton to Uganda:

> If economic reform seemed high on the agenda for Clinton's trip, it was not clear at all whether the same could be said of political reform. The issue is of prime importance precisely in those countries which are said to be led by the new generation of Africa's leaders. Key to these is Uganda, where people understandably wondered whether President Clinton's highly publicized support for President Yoweri Museveni may turn out to be at the expense of continuing political reform in the country.[392]

Overall, the United States has since the departure of Ambassador Michael Southwick been noticeably quiet about restrictions associated with the movement system. The few informal and unpublicized meetings which have taken place between U.S. officials and opposition politicians have done little to dispel the widely held view that the U.S. government is the patron of the Museveni government, a view which has substantially increased the legitimacy with which this form of the one-party state is seen on the continent.

---

[392]Mahmood Mamdani, "What was that trip all about?," *The Monitor*, April 10, 1998, p. 31.

The European Union and its Member States

Like most other Western donor countries, the member nations of the European Union (E.U.) have remained remarkably silent on the issue of democratization and respect for human rights in Uganda. Several E.U. countries regularly send delegations to Uganda and funding ties between E.U. members and Uganda are extensive, but human rights and democratization is rarely part of the public agenda of E.U.-Uganda interaction.

However, the E.U. issued a strong and unprecedented statement on the need for democratization in Uganda following a stormy Consultative Group donor meeting in Kampala in December 1998. In the days preceding the donor meeting, as noted, President Museveni's brother Major General Salim Saleh and the minister in charge of privatization resigned from their positions following a fraud scandal; a parliamentary committee released a damaging report on privatization and corruption in Uganda; and the World Bank handed over a confidential report to the Ugandan government documenting twelve cases of high-level corruption. The donor meeting took place against the background of increasing concern among donors about Ugandan and Rwandan involvement in the conflict in the Democratic Republic of Congo.

In the statement presented by Austria to the Ugandan government at the closing of the meeting, the E.U. stated its commitment to following political developments in Uganda:

> The E.U. shall monitor developments between now and the referendum in 2000 very closely. In particular it shall be looking at the terms and applications of the Political Organizations Bill for the regulation of political parties which it hopes will be passed very soon; the Referendum Bill and the time provided to debate it; and Movement's structures and activities, in particular the revival of the Chaka-mchaka political education programme.... There should be freedom of association in support of preferred candidates.

During a visit to Kampala, Irish Minister of State for Overseas Development and Human Rights, Liz O'Donnell, vowed that Ireland would support the referendum. The government's *New Vision* newspaper stated that O'Donnell declined to comment on the movement system of government but then asked: "What could be fairer than putting it to the people in 2000? If there is anything we can do to help, we will."[393]

---

[393]"Ireland to help on referendum," *New Vision*, June 4, 1998.

Nick Sigler, the British ruling Labour Party's secretary for international affairs, expressed concern over the movement system while attending an October 1997 conference of the Africa Multiparty Democracy Workshop sponsored by the British Labour Party. Sigler described the movement system as "worrying" because parties could not carry out their normal functions. He further stated that the referendum was a "cause for concern" because it would lead to the end of pluralism without putting into place another similarly competitive system.[394]

His comments contrasted with those of British Secretary of State for International Development Clare Short, who announced during a visit to Kampala in October 1997 that the British Labour government would not press for multiparty reforms in Uganda and that Britain would support the referendum:

> Uganda creates new optimism for Africa. The new British government likes to work with this kind of government. Our relationship with Uganda is precious. I do not think it is necessarily right for Uganda to have the same kind of political system as Britain.[395]

When the Ugandan Parliament was considering the proposed referendum legislation, the British High Commissioner to Uganda Michael Cook argued in favor of allowing political parties to campaign on the referendum issue, stating that "it is important for political parties to be given a proper platform to explain their cause before the referendum."[396] Thus, the United Kingdom has focused its attention on ensuring the procedural fairness of the referendum, ignoring the more basic concerns about the legitimacy of a referendum which puts fundamental human rights up for a vote.

A Star Pupil, Sheltered by the Word Bank?

The World Bank has been one of the strongest international supporters of President Museveni. President Museveni is one of the few allies of the World Bank on a continent increasingly dissatisfied with the bank's approach to structural adjustment and debt relief. Having invested heavily in making Uganda an economic success story, the World Bank is loathe to see Museveni criticized.

The relationship between Uganda and the World Bank is a symbiotic one, providing important benefits to both. Uganda is one of the few African countries

---

[394]John Kakande, "DP hosts African parties," *New Vision*, October 28, 1997.

[395]Erich Ogoso Opolot, "Britain will not press for parties," *New Vision*, October 7, 1997.

[396]"UK Envoy Appeals on Referendum," *New Vision*, June 25, 1999.

which has been willing to embrace the stringent structural adjustment programs which the World Bank considers essential to restoring fiscal discipline and monetary stability, and has served as an important advocate for the World Bank's programs in Africa. In January 1998, Uganda hosted a landmark closed-door meeting between World Bank president James Wolfensohn and leaders of twelve African countries to discuss the World Bank's policies in Africa.[397] Uganda has benefited from close attention from the World Bank and a generous economic package.

Uganda's economy has rebounded from a complete collapse in the 1970s and 1980s, and between 1994 and 1997 Uganda posted a real GDP growth rate of 8 percent, the highest in Africa. Because of its strict adherence to the fiscal discipline requirements and its sound economic reform record, Uganda was the first country to benefit from the Heavily Indebted Poor Countries (HIPC) initiative. In April 1998, the World Bank and the International Monetary Fund agreed to a U.S. $650 million debt relief package for Uganda, effectively reducing Uganda's external debt by twenty percent.[398] Since 1987, the World Bank has provided an estimated U.S. $790 million in adjustment support, in addition to an estimated U.S. $1 billion in project support in the agriculture, infrastructure, and social sectors.

Unfortunately, despite its recent commitment to "good governance," the World Bank has done little to address the need for political reform in Uganda. Its own assessments of the Ugandan government argue that "economic reform has been accompanied by political reform," and that the Ugandan government is "composed of broad-based political groupings brought together under the country's no-party political system."[399] The World Bank has touted Uganda's economic achievements and ignored its civil and political rights shortcomings, thereby playing a counterproductive role in Uganda's democratization process.

The willingness of the World Bank and key donors to ignore Uganda's rights problems was clearly demonstrated at the most recent Consultative Group Meeting in Kampala in December 1998. The donor meeting took place at a time that Uganda, together with Rwanda, was openly embroiled in the conflict in the neighboring Democratic Republic of Congo, aiming to topple the government of Laurent Kabila, himself installed with Ugandan and Rwandan support. On

---

[397]Stephen Buckley, "African Leaders Ask World Bank for More Aid," *Washington Post*, January 25, 1998.

[398]Press Release, "Uganda to receive U.S. $650 million in debt relief," *The World Bank Group*, April 8, 1998.

[399]"Countries: Uganda,"   from   the   World   Bank   website   at http://www.worldbank.org/html/extdr/offrep/afr/ug2.htm.

December 8, days before the Consultative Group Meeting, the Ugandan Parliament released a damning report on Uganda's privatization process, arguing that privatization had been "derailed by corruption," and implicating three senior ministers who had "political responsibility." According to the report, most of the funds raised through privatization had apparently disappeared due to corruption. President Museveni's own brother and defense advisor, Major General Salim Saleh, had been forced to resign two days earlier after it was revealed that he had improperly and secretly tried to buy a majority stake in the Uganda Commercial Bank (UCB). The World Bank itself shared a confidential report detailing many cases of corruption involving government officials with the Ugandan government prior to the Consultative Group meeting, a report later released to the public at the request of the Ugandan government.[400] Despite these concerns and the continued moves towards a more restrictive political system, the Consultative Group Meeting ended with Uganda receiving its biggest-yet package of aid: U.S. $2.2 billion, to be dispersed over the next three years. A strong statement issued by the European Union at the end of the meeting, discussed above, was a strong indication of rising international concern about Uganda's restrictive political practices.

The World Bank's support for Uganda's economic rehabilitation may ignore one of the greatest threat to Uganda's economic recovery, namely corruption. It is difficult to track corruption in Uganda because of a lack of transparency by the government, at least partly caused by the limitations placed on political opposition and the repressive actions faced by politicians who try to raise corruption concerns. In the words of Aggrey Awori, an opposition Member of Parliament, the corruption is a symptom "of an unaccountable government. If there was an effective opposition based on party lines, that would hold them accountable and threaten their tenure as government."[401] With Uganda dependent on the international community for fifty-five percent of its budget, the international community and the World Bank certainly could do more to ensure the government of Uganda respects its international treaty obligations and fundamental human rights.

The Impact of the International Community's Lack of Resolve

By publicly ignoring the abuses of civil and political rights associated with the movement system in Uganda, the international community undermines the

---

[400]World Bank, Poverty Reduction and Social Development Section, "Uganda: Recommendations for Strengthening the Government of Uganda's Anti-Corruption Program," November 1998.

[401]Paul Busharizi, "Uganda under pressure to embrace more democracy," Reuters, January 15, 1999.

effectiveness of its work on human rights and democracy elsewhere on the continent. A message is being sent that the international community will be willing to tolerate significant abuses of human rights, as long as the government maintains some surface acceptability. But by turning a blind eye to the abuses committed under the movement system, it becomes more difficult to call for improved human rights records and increased democratization in other countries, as the very notion of the universality of human rights is undermined. Human rights then becomes a tool of foreign policy, used against one's enemies and ignored in the case of one's friends.

APPENDIX I: SELECTED ARTICLES FROM UGANDA'S CONSTITUTION (1995)

Chapter Four: Protection and Promotion of Fundamental and Other Human Rights and Freedoms

20 . (1) Fundamental rights and freedoms of the individual are inherent and not granted by the State.

(2) The rights and freedoms of the individual and groups enshrined in this Chapter shall be respected, upheld and promoted by all organs and agencies of Government and by all persons.

...

29.   (1) Every person shall have the right to—

(a) freedom of speech and expression, which shall include freedom of the press and other media;

(b) freedom of thought, conscience and belief, which shall include academic freedom in institutions of learning;

(c) freedom to practise any religion and manifest such practice which shall be include the right to belong to and participate in the practices of any religious body or organisation in a manner consistent with this Constitution;

(d) freedom to assemble and to demonstrate together with others peacefully and unarmed and to petition; and

(e) freedom of association which shall include the freedom to form and join associations or unions, including trade unions and political or other civic organizations.

...

38.   (1) Every Uganda citizen has the right to participate in the affairs of government, individually or through his or her representatives in accordance with law.

(2) Every Ugandan has a right to participate in peaceful activities to influence the policies of government through civic organizations.

...

Chapter Five: Representation of the People

69.   (1) The people of Uganda shall have the right to choose and adopt a political system of their choice through free and fair elections or referenda.

(2) The political systems referred to in clause (1) of this article shall include—

(a)   the movement political system;

(b)   the multi-party political system; and

(c)   any other democratic and representative political system.

70.   (1) The movement political system is broad based, inclusive and non-partisan and shall conform to the following principles—

(a)   participatory democracy;

(b)   democracy, accountability and transparency;

(c)   accessibility to all positions of leadership by all citizens;

(d)   individual merit as a basis for election to political offices.

(2) Parliament may—

(a)   create organs under the movement political system and define their roles; and

(b)   prescribe from time to time, any other democratic principle of the movement political system, as it may consider necessary.

71.   A political party in the multi-party political system shall conform to the following principles—

(a) every political party shall have a national character;

(b) membership of a political party shall not be based on sex, ethnicity, religion, or other sectional division;

(c) the internal organisation of a political party shall conform to the democratic principles enshrined in this Constitution;

(d) members of the national organs of a political party shall be regularly elected from citizens of Uganda in conformity with the provisions of paragraphs (a) and (b) of this article and with due consideration for gender;

(e) political parties shall be required by law to account for the sources and use of their funds and assets;

(f) no person shall be compelled to join a particular political party by virtue of belonging to an organisation or interest group.

72. (1) Subject to the provisions of this Constitution, the right to form political parties and any other political organisations is guaranteed.

(2) An organisation shall not operate as a political party or organisation unless it conforms to the principles laid down in this Constitution and it is registered.

(3) Parliament shall by law regulate the financing and functioning of political organisations.

73. (1) Subject to the provisions of this Constitution, but notwithstanding the provisions of paragraph (e) of clause (1) of article 29 and article 43 of this Constitution, during the period when any of the political systems provided for in this Constitution has been adopted, organisations subscribing to other political systems may exist subject to such regulations as Parliament shall by law prescribe.

(2) Regulations prescribed under this article shall not exceed what is necessary for enabling the political system adopted to operate.

74.   (1) A referendum shall be held for the purpose of changing the political
       system—

       (a)   if requested by a resolution supported by more than half of all
              members of Parliament; or

       (b)   if requested by a resolution supported by the majority of the total
              membership of each of at least one half of all district councils; or

       (c)   if requested through a petition to the Electoral Commission by at
              least one-tenth of the registered voters from at each of at least two-
              thirds of the constituencies for which representatives are required
              to be directly elected under paragraph (a) of clause (1) of article 78
              of this Constitution.

       (2) The political system may also be changed by the elected representatives
       of the people in Parliament and district councils by resolution of
       Parliament supported by not less than two thirds of all members of
       Parliament upon a petition to it supported by not less than two thirds
       majority of the total membership of each of at least half of all district
       councils.

       (3) The resolutions or petitions for the purposes of changing the political
       system shall be taken only in the fourth year of the term of any
       Parliament.

75.   Parliament shall have no power to enact a law establishing a one-party state.

                                     ...

Chapter Nineteen: Transitional Provisions

269. On the commencement of this Constitution and until Parliament makes laws
     regulating the activities of political organisations in accordance with article
     73 of this Constitution, political activities may continue except—

     (a) opening and operating branch offices;

     (b) holding delegates' conferences;

(c) holding public rallies;

(d) sponsoring or offering a platform to or in any way campaigning for or against a candidate for any public elections;

(e) carrying on any activities that may interfere with the movement political system for the time being in force.

270. Notwithstanding the provisions of clause (2) of article 72 of this Constitution, but subject to article 269 of this Constitution, the political parties or organisations in existence immediately before the coming into force of this Constitution shall continue to exist and operate in conformity with the provisions of this Constitution until Parliament makes laws relating to registration of political parties and organisations.

271. (1) Notwithstanding the provisions of article 69 of this Constitution, the first presidential, parliamentary, local government and other public elections after the promulgation of this Constitution shall be held under the movement political system.

(2) Two years before the expiry of the term of the first Parliament elected under this Constitution, any person shall be free to canvas for public support for a political system of his or her choice for purposes of a referendum.

(3) During the last month of the fourth year of the term of Parliament referred to in clause (2) of this article, a referendum shall be held to determine the political system the people of Uganda wish to adopt.

(4) Parliament shall enact laws to give effect to the provisions of this article.

APPENDIX II: SELECTED ARTICLES OF THE UGANDA PENAL CODE

Chapter VII: Treason and Offences Against the State

25. [Treason]
    (1) Any person who,

      (a)   levies war against the Republic of Uganda;

      (b)   unlawfully causes or attempt to cause the death of the President or, with intent to maim or disfigure or disable, unlawfully wounds or does any harm to the person of the President, or aims at the person of the President any gun, offensive weapon, pistol or any description of firearms, whether the same contains any explosive or destructive substance or not;

      (c)   contrives any plot, act or matter and expresses or declares such plot, act or matter by any utterance or by any overt act in order, by force of arms, to overturn the Government as by law established;

      (d)   aids or abets another person in the commission of the foregoing acts, or becomes an accessory before or after the fact to any of the foregoing acts, or conceals any of the foregoing acts,

commits an offence and shall suffer death.

    (2) Any person who forms an intention to effect any of the following purposes, that is to say,

      (a)   to compel by force or constraint the Government as by law established to change its measures or counsels or to intimidate or overawe the National Assembly; or

      (b)   to instigate any person to invade the Republic of Uganda with an armed force, and manifest any such intention by an overt act or by any utterance or by publishing any printing or writing,

commits an offence and shall suffer death.

(3) Any person who advisedly attempts to affect any of the following purposes, that is to say,

    (a)   to incite any person to commit an act of mutiny or any treacherous or mutinous act; or

    (b)   to incite any such person to make or endeavor to make a mutinous assembly,

commits an offence and shall be liable to suffer death.

...

27. [Concealment of Treason]
    Any person who,

(a) (repealed by Act 29 of 1970, section 1(c)),

(b) knowing that any person intends to commit treason does not give information thereof with all reasonable despatch to the Minister, an administrative officer, a magistrate or an officer in charge of a police station, or use all reasonable endeavours to prevent the commission of the offence of treason,

commits the offence of misprision of treason, and shall be liable on conviction to imprisonment for life.

28. [Terrorism]
    (1) Any person who engages in or carries out acts of terrorism is guilty of an offence and is liable to imprisonment for life.

    (2) Any person who aids, finances, harbours or in any other way renders support to any other person, knowing or having reason to believe that such support will be applied or used for or in connection with the commission, preparation or instigation of acts of terrorism is guilty of an offence and is liable to imprisonment for life.

    (3) Any person who cither,

(a)   belongs or professes to belong to a terrorist organisation; or

(b)   solicits or invites financial or other support for a terrorist organisation, or knowingly makes or receives any contribution of money or otherwise to the resources of a terrorist organisation,

is guilty of an offence and is liable to imprisonment for ten years: provided that a person belonging to a terrorist organisation shall not be guilty of an offence under this subsection by reason of belonging to the organisation if he shows that he became a member when it was not a terrorist organisation and that he has not since he became a member taken part in any of its activities at any time while it was a terrorist organisation.

(4) Without prejudice to the right to adduce evidence in rebuttal, any person who imports, sells, distributes, manufactures or is in the possession of any firearm, explosives or ammunition without a valid licence or reasonable excuse shall be deemed to be engaged in acts of terrorism.

(5) The Minister responsible for internal security may, with the prior approval of the Cabinet, declare any organisation engaged in or carrying out acts of terrorism to be a terrorist organisation for the purposes of this section.

(6) In this section the word "terrorism" means the use of violence or threat thereof with intent to promote or achieve political ends in an unlawful manner and includes the use of violence or threat thereof calculated to put the public in such fear as may cause discontent against the government.

...

41. [Seditious Intention]
    (1) A seditious intention shall be an intention—

(a)   to bring into hatred or contempt or to excite disaffection against the person of the President, the Government as by law established or the Constitution;

(b)   to excite any person to attempt to procure the alteration, otherwise than by lawful means, of any matter of State as by law established;

(c)   to bring into hatred or contempt or to excite disaffection against the administration of justice;

(d)   to raise discontent or disaffection among any body or group of persons;

(e)   to promote feelings of ill-will and hostility, religious animosity or communal ill-feeling among any body or group of persons;

(f)   (repealed by Statutory Instrument 135 of 1968);

(g)   to subvert or promote the subversion of the Government or the Administration of a District.

(2) For the purposes of this section an act, speech or publication shall not be deemed to be seditious by reason only that it intends—

(a)   to show that the Government has been misled or mistaken in any of its measures;

(b)   to point out errors or defects in the Government or the Constitution, or in legislation or in the administration of justice with a view to the remedying of such errors or defects;

(c)   to persuade any person to attempt to procure by lawful means the alteration of any matters as by law established; or

(d)   to point out, with a view to their removal, any matters which are producing or have a tendency to produce feelings of ill-will and anmity among anybody or group of persons.

(3) (Consequently repealed by Statutory Instrument 135 of 1968.)

(4) For the purposes of this section in determining whether the intention with which any act was done, any words were spoken, or any document was published, was or was not seditious, every person shall be deemed to intend the consequences which would naturally follow from his conduct at the time and in the circumstances in which he was conducting himself.